International Sports Betting

Sports betting has become a truly global phenomenon, facilitated by new communication technologies. As a result, the development of deviances, from match-fixing to money laundering, has accelerated. This new reality has numerous implications, for both the regulation of this billion-dollar industry and the very integrity of sport, sport financing and betting operations.

Written by an international team of academic researchers and industry professionals, *International Sports Betting* explores the central concepts of integrity and deviance, governance and policy, as well as perennial issues linked to the gambling sector, such as regulatory responsibilities and the fight against gambling addiction. Unlike other treatments of the gambling industry, the book offers a multi-disciplinary sociological and managerial critique that goes beyond a traditional focus on law and regulation.

This is fascinating reading for any student, researcher or practitioner working in the areas of sport business, international business, international regulation, policy studies or gambling studies.

Jean-Patrick Villeneuve is Vice-Dean of the Faculty of Communication Sciences, Associate Professor and Director of the Institute for Public Communication at the Università della Svizzera italiana, Switzerland. He also has appointments in Canada (ENAP), France (University of Pau) and China (UIBE). He currently sits on the Independent Expert Panel of the Open Government Partnership.

Martial Pasquier is Vice-Rector of the University of Lausanne, Switzerland and Professor of Public Management at the Swiss Graduate School of Public Administration (IDHEAP). He sits on numerous Boards and Foundation Councils.

Routledge Research in Sport Business and Management

Available in this series:

4) **Organisational Performance Management in Sport**
   Ian O'Boyle

5) **Sport in Latin America**
   Policy, organisation, management
   Edited by Gonzalo Bravo, Rosa Lopez de D'Amico and Charles Parrish

6) **Sports Agents and Labour Markets**
   Evidence from world football
   Giambattista Rossi, Anna Semens and Jean Francois Brochard

7) **Managing Drugs in Sport**
   Jason Mazanov

8) **Elite Youth Sport Policy and Management**
   A comparative analysis
   Edited by Elsa Kristiansen, Milena M. Parent and Barrie Houlihan

9) **Women in Sport Leadership**
   Research and practice for change
   Edited by Laura J. Burton and Sarah Leberman

10) **International Sports Betting**
    Integrity, deviance, governance and policy
    Edited by Jean-Patrick Villeneuve and Martial Pasquier

International Sports Betting
Integrity, Deviance, Governance and Policy

Edited by Jean-Patrick Villeneuve and Martial Pasquier

LONDON AND NEW YORK

First published 2019
by Routledge
2 Park Square, Milton Park, Abingdon, Oxon OX14 4RN

and by Routledge
711 Third Avenue, New York, NY 10017

Routledge is an imprint of the Taylor & Francis Group, an informa business

© 2019 selection and editorial matter, Jean-Patrick Villeneuve and Martial Pasquier; individual chapters, the contributors

The right of Jean-Patrick Villeneuve and Martial Pasquier to be identified as the authors of the editorial material, and of the authors for their individual chapters, has been asserted in accordance with sections 77 and 78 of the Copyright, Designs and Patents Act 1988.

All rights reserved. No part of this book may be reprinted or reproduced or utilised in any form or by any electronic, mechanical, or other means, now known or hereafter invented, including photocopying and recording, or in any information storage or retrieval system, without permission in writing from the publishers.

Trademark notice: Product or corporate names may be trademarks or registered trademarks, and are used only for identification and explanation without intent to infringe.

British Library Cataloguing-in-Publication Data
A catalogue record for this book is available from the British Library

Library of Congress Cataloging-in-Publication Data
A catalog record has been requested for this book

ISBN: 978-1-138-78475-8 (hbk)
ISBN: 978-1-315-76817-5 (ebk)

Typeset in Times New Roman
by Out of House Publishing

Contents

List of contributors   vi

Introduction – sports betting: a series of transversal challenges   1
JEAN-PATRICK VILLENEUVE AND MARTIAL PASQUIER

1   Canada's regulatory framework for sports betting: a fragmented reality   5
JEAN-FRANÇOIS SAVARD

2   Multidimensional performance of sports betting operators   27
LEA MEYER

3   Cases of match-fixing in tennis and snooker   42
DAWN AQUILINA

4   Match fixing and money laundering   64
JACK ANDERSON

5   Integrity challenges for protection of minors: Australian compromises on sports broadcasting betting advertising   79
LINDA HANCOCK

Index   103

Contributors

Jack Anderson is Professor and Director of Sports Law, Melbourne Law School, University of Melbourne.

Dawn Aquilina is Senior Lecturer at the University of Malta, Malta.

Linda Hancock is Professor of Politics and Policy Studies at Deakin University, Australia.

Lea Meyer is Director of Polaris Strategic Foresight, consulting regulators and operators of the international gaming industry in performance, management and regulation.

Jean-François Savard is Professor of Public Policy Analysis and Development at the École nationale d'administration publique, Canada.

Introduction

Sports betting: a series of transversal challenges

Jean-Patrick Villeneuve and Martial Pasquier

Gambling is historically linked to divination: the desire to know and anticipate future events. The possibilities to gamble have since greatly evolved; from the relatively simple game of dice played by Roman soldiers to the current online sports betting offer. That said, the fundamental logic is unchanged: the desire to wager on the occurrence or not of a future event.

This particular activity has a transversal role in society: it is an economic sector, a popular form of entertainment, a source of financial revenue for states and much more. It is when coupled with another important social activity, sport, that gambling takes on its most diverse, complex and involved nature.

This short collection of contributions presents some of these transversal logics of sport betting. Each of the chapters addresses specific and central questions. Jean-François Savard approaches the topic from a regulatory perspective, examining the way in which territories limit and control the possibilities to gamble. Lea Meyer traces the finality and objectives of the organisations allowed to operate under the given regulation of a territory or state. Dawn Aquilina discusses the issue of sport deviances, specifically the development of match-fixing schemes to ensure specific outcomes and therefore guarantee a winning bet. Jack Anderson looks at the use of revenues derived from betting schemes by organised crime. Finally, Linda Hancock considers the addictive nature of gambling, notably for young players in the context of slack regulation of sports betting advertising.

The framework that limits and controls the provision of gambling services in a specific context can take several forms. While few national regulations ban gambling outright (Pakistan, for example), none gives it a completely free hand. Most jurisdictions, depending on their history, culture, society and institutional construct, find different arbitrages to allow some aspects of gambling, while banning others. The 'maître d'oeuvre' of this regulation is in some instances local while in other jurisdictions national. At times regulations cover all forms of gambling and in others differentiates among them.

In Chapter 1, Jean-François Savard takes Canada as an example of the development of regulatory frameworks. He positions the importance of the political form, federalism, and its impact on the regulation of sports betting. He identifies different models of regulation used in the Canadian context, differentiating between 'joint venture' approaches, where private contractors operate, 'charitable' approaches, where charitable and religious organisations are active and 'government ownership and controls', where public corporations are the main actors. With the multiplication of regulatory models within the same country, Savard poses the question of regulatory fragmentation and its consequences, notably the coherence of the Canadian model. This contribution provides a grid to better understand and analyse the various options to the necessary regulation of sports betting.

In Chapter 2, Lea Meyer addresses a related issue to that of regulation: the way in which sport-betting providers define their role and objectives in a given regulatory environment. While private sector organisations strive for profit in a marketplace of products and services, public institutions have had to provide broader and more multiverse definitions of their objectives. That central question of the nature of organisations, is posed in the decidedly mixed environment of sports betting where organisations, public or private, will offer products that are not only similar but in many instances exactly the same, i.e. the offer of a bet on a specific game. Far from focusing exclusively on financial returns, Meyer posits that six elements, ranging from stakeholder dimensions to social issues and public values, are essential for defining the performance of sports betting providers. She posits that responsible gaming is, and must be, central. She addresses these categories by looking at the cases of the Belgian and Norwegian lotteries. These underline why regulation is essential in the field of sports betting, linking it to Savard's contribution, but also presenting some of the key deviances a broader definition of performance must necessarily address.

Dawn Aquilina, in Chapter 3, looks at one such deviance, the fixing of sport matches, i.e. the act of 'illegally influencing the course or the result of a sporting competition in order to obtain an advantage for oneself or for others' (Brasseur, 2012: 6). Her chapter considers the causes and consequences of match-fixing from the point of view of sport itself. By looking at two highly mediatised and betting-intensive sports, tennis and snooker, she brings into focus several elements that enable deviances to emerge in the first place. Match-fixing jeopardises first and foremost the integrity of sport: the fact that the outcome of any sport event can be known in advance defeats the very purpose of it taking place. This insidious development touches upon the very heart of what sport is in modern society: entertainment and business, but also a social symbol, a way of connecting increasingly diverse societies and territories. It is for that reason that match-fixing has been labelled one of the most serious and insidious threats to sport. Reporting and prosecuting have been the main approaches used to address this challenge. But, as Aquilina underlines, educating players and other stakeholders in sport is a precondition for restoring trust and faith in sports as an essential social activity.

The development of match-fixing would not have taken its current dimension if it were not for the active involvement of criminal organisations. In Chapter 4, Jack Anderson addresses the use of sports betting by criminal organisations to launder the benefits of crime. Starting by defining what exactly is meant by money-laundering, the chapter then presents the now long-standing interest organised crime has in gambling, notably through the analysis of the 1950s US Senate Special Committee to Investigate Organised Crime in Interstate Commerce, better known as the Kefauver Committee. Moving from the political realm to the sport realm, the 2009 report on money-laundering through football, published by the multilateral Financial Action Task Force is analysed to identify the vulnerabilities of sport in this sector as well as the almost seamless integration of criminal logics within sports betting. Anderson's analysis comes to a clear conclusion: the challenges raised by the money-laundering of the benefits of sports betting activities and the corollary match-fixing deviances, cannot be solved by sport alone. He presents three key recommendations to enable sport to more effectively address the issue in collaboration with other stakeholders.

The last, and for many the essential problem related to sports betting, is the addictive nature of the activity and the ensuing development of problem gambling; especially with the development of new online technologies that facilitate remote betting. In Chapter 5, Linda Hancock addresses the protection of young players in the Australian context of controversies over sports betting advertising during broadcast sporting events. The protection of players from the potentially addictive nature of gambling has been integrated in all regulatory frameworks. The digitisation of sports betting offers have made betting possibilities more numerous and flexible, offering gambling opportunities 24 hours per day and from any location imaginable. The challenge of protecting players, especially minors, is heightened in such an environment. Hancock analyses the sports betting advertisement reforms implemented in Australia through the use of a corporate political activity framework. The case study shows that the current environment, with the multiplication of advertising forms and platforms, is 'messy and difficult to regulate' and the 'enforcement is complex and untested'. The compromises reached in the Australian case for the advertisement of sport-betting offers, points to the underlying transversal nature of sports betting. The issue of player protection had to be negotiated with other actors and by taking into account other dynamics, more financial and economic than social. The example illustrates the ongoing power of vested financial and political interests over public interest concerns about the creeping expansion and promotion of new forms of gambling and the potentially damaging impact on young people.

1 Canada's regulatory framework for sports betting

A fragmented reality

Jean-François Savard

A century ago, most forms of gambling were unlawful in Canada, and considered vices (Campbell & Smith, 1998). But the regulatory framework has greatly evolved since 1892, when the Criminal Code first declared a complete ban on gambling activities (Azmier, Jepson & Patton, 1999). Over the years, periodic amendments were made to the Criminal Code that slowly eroded this blanket ban. Minor adjustments between 1892 and 1969 facilitated the gradual expansion of gambling activities (Campbell & Smith, 1998): charitable gambling was permitted in 1900, pari-mutuel betting on horse racing in 1910, and gambling events at agricultural fairs and exhibitions in 1925 (Azmier et al., 1999). In 1969, the Criminal Code was substantially amended to allow federal and provincial governments to enter the field of gambling (Azmier et al., 1999). Provincial governments established their own activities, which considerably altered the gambling landscape. At the same time, the federal government created Lotto Canada and the Sports Pool Corporation – primarily to fund the upcoming Summer Olympics, held in Montreal in 1976 (Osborne & Campbell, 1988).

But in 1979, facing strong opposition from the provincial governments, the conservative federal government agreed to cease Lotto Canada activities; and it formally transferred all such powers to provincial legislatures. This agreement took several years to be enforced: it was rejected in 1980 by the newly elected liberal government. Only in 1985, when a conservative government was again in power, was the arrangement formalised (Osborne & Campbell, 1988). According to Osborne and Campbell, Parliament 'divested the federal government of any capacity to conduct lotteries', leaving the provinces with 'sole jurisdiction over lotteries and other specific gaming operations' (Osborne & Campbell, 1988: p. 24). In exchange for the federal government relinquishing its responsibilities for gaming regulations, operations and revenues, the provincial governments agreed to contribute $100 million to the Calgary Winter Olympics in 1988 (Azmier et al., 1999).

These changes reflect four major trends in gambling policies in Canada. First came a transition in the official view of gambling, from criminalisation to legalisation. What followed was a pattern of lesser federal involvement, and greater provincial authority. An increase in new gambling products came next; and finally an expansion of gambling activities, driven by interest groups (Campbell & Smith, 2003). The most important of these changes was the 1985 amendment of the Criminal Code, which permitted the provinces to conduct and manage gaming. This opened the field not only to regular lotteries and other traditional activities, but also to video lottery terminals and forms of electronic gambling – including, more recently, internet gambling.

What explains these trends? The main reasons are economic. Gambling in Canada was advocated not so much for its own sake – as a 'harmless and worthwhile recreation' – than as an activity that successfully '[serves] a greater good, such as generating government revenues, funding charity, [and] creating jobs' (Campbell & Smith, 1998: p. 24). For instance, confronted with the expenses of funding the 1967 World's Fair and the 1976 Olympic Games in Montreal, the Québec government saw in gambling a revenue opportunity to ease those burdens (Azmier et al., 1999). In the 1990s other provincial governments also saw gambling as an easy and painless way to extract new revenues, as they faced both an economic recession and a federal downloading of fiscal responsibilities (Black, 1996). The provinces also perceived Lotto Canada as inefficient (Osborne, 1989), and felt that the federal government was draining revenues that should properly have been allocated to them. These tensions were resolved by the 1985 Criminal Code amendments, and the dismantling of Lotto Canada the same year.

This chapter provides an overview of sports-betting regulations in Canada, and analyses the coherence of the framework. Although the social impacts of sports betting (such as criminality, addiction, urban development, etc.) are important ones, and should be addressed, we do not focus on them here. Nor do we cover the fiscal advantages or disadvantages.

Understanding Canadian federalism

Sports-betting regulations in Canada reflect the nature and complexity of this country's government – which we might call a dualistic federalism. Many authors (such as Burgess, 1993; Gibbins, 1987; McRoberts, 1993; and Watts, 1998) maintain that Canada is in fact a highly decentralised federation. In some respects, this is true; however, our federation is not so much decentralised as shared. Indeed, Sections 91 to 95 of Canada's 1867 Constitutional Act (in many respects a bizarrely hybrid document[1]) outline which legislative powers are exclusive to the federal government, and which to the provincial governments. Both levels can only pass legislation or implement policies on matters that fall under their respective powers. The only two areas of shared jurisdiction are agriculture and immigration; but even there, a federal act or policy always takes precedence over a provincial one. Canada has no form of executive federalism or inter-delegation (from the federal to the provincial level), as exists (for instance) in Switzerland, Germany or Australia.

This might give rise to the idea that Canada has very little collaboration or dialogue between the levels of government. In fact, since the 1970s the Canadian political landscape has been characterised by intense intergovernmental relations. At different times, these relations have been either friendly or adversarial – sometimes both at once, depending on viewpoint. A prime example was the Social Union Framework Agreement of 1999 – an intergovernmental agreement that defined the quality of social programmes offered by the provinces. Since the federal government had no jurisdiction over such social programmes, Prime Minister Jean Chrétien proposed to support the provinces financially if they respected the federal principles. It took months of intense negotiations before the provinces and territories agreed; the only holdout was Québec, which felt that the agreement infringed on its constitutional rights.

Clearly, intergovernmental tensions are a common force for change in Canadian public policies; and the field of gambling is no exception. Pressure from the provinces caused the system to evolve from the federal government having sole responsibility – which it did in 1892 by simply forbidding the activity – to a complex web of federal and provincial regulations across the country.

Regulatory framework for sports betting

The federal Criminal Code defines gambling as a game of chance, or a mix of chance and skill (Bowal & Carrasco, 1997). Canada's gambling regulations are based on 11 parts of the Code: Sections 197, and 201 to 209. The first of these defines the terms 'bet' and 'game', as well as the locations where gaming can occur; these include 'public place', 'common betting house', 'common gaming house', and the charmingly old-fashioned 'disorderly house' (Campbell, Hartnagel & Smith, 2005; Canada, 2015). Sections 201 to 203, plus 206, define as criminal offences the operating of betting, lotteries and gambling (including casinos). However, Sections 204 and 207 provide exemptions that legalise certain activities. Pari-mutuel wagers on trotting or pacing horse-races are legal, as long as the races are conducted by an agency licensed by the Minister of Agriculture and Agri-Food Canada (as per Section 204). And lottery and gambling activities are lawful if they are operated by a provincial government; or by a charitable or religious organisation, fair or exhibition that is licensed by a provincial government, as per Section 207 (Campbell et al., 2005; Canada, 2015).

In Canada, formal betting on the outcome of specific sports events is officially illegal. Section 201 of the Criminal Code prohibits the establishment of common gaming or betting houses; and Sections 202 and 203 prohibit book-making, pool-selling, betting, placing or agreeing to make a bet (Bowal & Carrasco, 1997). However, Section 204 provides certain exemptions, such as for private bets between not more than ten individuals. Horse racing is also exempted, as indicated above (Bowal & Carrasco, 1997). Canadians can legally bet on horse racing at any licensed race tracks, and privately in small groups as long as the bets are not part of any formal scheme.

But what about sports betting – is it never legal in Canada? To answer that question, we must shed more light on the regulatory framework. The exemptions laid out in the Criminal Code permit provincial governments the right to operate, regulate and control legalised gambling activities such as lotteries (Azmier & Smith, 1998); but not betting activities. This makes it impossible 'for there to be gambling in Canada without the direct involvement of provincial governments, either through licensing, regulating or directly operating' (Azmier, Jepson & Patton, 1999: p. 4).

The consequence of this is that each province has its own regulations for licensing authorised gambling activities (Bowal & Carrasco, 1997). The provincial governments can delegate licensing power to bodies such as municipalities and First Nations communities. They may also subcontract the day-to-day operations of gambling activities – such as casinos, bingos, and electronic and internet gambling – to private operators, though lotteries may not be subcontracted (Azmier et al., 1999). Horse racing remains a federal power, and sports betting remains unlawful.

However, Section 207 of the Criminal Code contains a loophole in the law, which many provincial governments ingeniously took advantage of: they created lotteries to run sports betting. The catch is that to be considered a lottery, such schemes do not allow players to bet on a single event – they must buy a ticket allowing them to gamble on a series of results or matches. Such sports-betting lotteries are regulated and operated by a complex web of regulatory and operational bodies across the country. They are, in fact, 'overseen by provincial governments, and marketed and distributed collaboratively by a cartel of provincial agencies' (Campbell & Smith, 1998: p. 25).

Governance of the sector in the provinces includes the power to regulate and implement gambling as the provincial governments see fit. However, it is worth noting that many have separated the agencies that licence gambling activities, and those that actually conduct them. Two reasons might explain this choice. On the one hand, 'the rapid expansion of gambling creates the need for larger and more specialised agencies, whose functions may be better achieved if divided'. On the other hand, 'dividing the operator and regulator functions helps the provinces avoid potential conflicts of interest' (Azmier et al., 1999: p. 4).

This splitting-up means that the gambling sector in Canada is characterised by a patchwork of regulations – an unsurprising outcome, given that regulations, operations and available games vary from one province to another (Campbell et al., 2005). This result is explained by the autonomy the Criminal Code offers to the provinces, and by the natural political instinct to borrow good ideas. Provinces are free to develop their own regulations, but also to pick and choose from each other's (Azmier et al., 1999). This results in a number of inconsistencies across the country: 'the type of gambling available, the disbursement of provincial revenues from gambling, the return to players, etc., differ from one jurisdiction to the next' (Azmier & Smith, 1998: p. 1). In addition, provinces may band together and create regional organisations. The Atlantic Lottery Corporation, for instance, is a joint creation by the governments of Newfoundland and Labrador, Nova Scotia, New Brunswick and Prince Edward Island. There is also a pan-Canadian agency that operates a national lottery, Interprovincial Lottery Corporation (which include sports betting). All these organisations are based on provincial agreements, which in turn are based on provincial regulations.

From this complex patchwork of regulations, three recurring approaches emerge. We might term these the Joint-Venture model, the Charitable model and the Government Ownership and Operation model (Campbell et al., 2005; Campbell & Smith, 1998). The first of these, the joint-venture model, involves provincial government and charities entering into contractual arrangements with private operators to run parts of gambling activities (Azmier et al., 1999). This kind of arrangement can take two forms. The province, as regulator and licensing authority, might contract a private enterprise to provide gaming installations, and to supervise their operation, for instance providing slot machines in a Casino and maintaining them, without running the actual gambling operation. Alternatively, the province might contract the private enterprise to provide gaming services and products directly to the gambling population (Campbell et al., 2005). Examples of such joint ventures in Canada are almost entirely limited to casinos.

The second model is charitable. All Canadian provinces issue licences for charitable organisations to run gambling activities (Campbell et al., 2005). This even includes some forms of sports betting, provided that these respect provincial regulations by taking the form of lotteries. Usually provincial licences are issued only for short periods, and for small-scale events (Campbell & Smith, 1998); and the profits can only be used for charitable or religious purposes (Azmier, 2005; Campbell et al., 2005). However, enforcement of these activities is almost impossible, since they are 'extremely difficult to track and measure'. Licensing of such charitable activities 'is sometimes done via thousands of municipalities; and provinces only track the largest events' (Azmier, 2005: p. 3).

The government ownership and operation model is straightforward: the province controls everything, through state agencies. The best example of this is Québec's Liquor, Racing and Gaming Commission (Régie des alcools, des courses et des jeux), which has the broad mandate of regulating not just gambling but also horse racing and liquor licenses (including organisations and events). Another provincial authority is Loto-Québec, which owns and operates all casinos in the province, and conducts lotteries and electronic gambling. However, it is not responsible for charitable events, which would be conducted by charitable organisations and regulated by the Régie des alcools, des courses et des jeux. In Québec, the private sector is not completely absent from the gambling industry, but its participation is limited. Apart from small-scale charitable events that allow private contractors to lease equipment and provide staff, Loto-Québec limits the private sector to the distribution of lottery tickets, through an elaborate system of retailers across the province. Sports betting is limited to province-run lotteries.

As mentioned earlier, *regional* lottery corporations increase the complexity of the gambling landscape. There are currently two such non-profit bodies in Canada: the Atlantic Lottery Corporation, and the Western Canada Lottery Corporation. These own the equipment on their territories; create and operate lotteries (including video lotteries); contract with retailers to distribute lottery tickets; and market and promote their products (Campbell et al., 2005). Under the umbrella of the regional corporation, each province is responsible for its own gambling activities. In Nova Scotia, for example, the government's Alcohol and Gaming Division regulates the sector and licenses operators. In New Brunswick, the Gaming Control Branch of the Department of Public Safety performs the same function; while the Lotteries and Gaming Corporations oversees the province's Responsible Gaming policy. It also manages agreements with the service providers that operate casinos, and acts as the province's shareholder in the Atlantic Lottery Corporation.

In Prince Edward Island, the Department of Justice and Public Safety licenses and regulates charitable events and organisations, while two Lotteries Commissions regulate lotteries and electronic gaming activities. The regulation of casinos in the province, however, is left to the Atlantic Lottery Corporation. Finally, in Newfoundland and Labrador, lotteries and electronic gaming are regulated by the Department of Public Safety, and operated by the Atlantic Lottery Corporation. However, charitable events and organisations are regulated and licensed by the Department of Government Services.

At the other end of the country, the Western Canada Lottery Corporation operates lotteries, games and related activities on behalf of Alberta, Saskatchewan and Manitoba. Marketing is done in collaboration with provincial organisations: the Alberta Gaming and Liquor Commission, Saskatchewan Lotteries and the Manitoba Liquor and Lotteries Corporation. Alberta's Commission administers the Gaming and Liquor Act, and thus regulates gambling; it is also the licensing body for casinos, bingos and lotteries, as well as for charitable and non-profit organisations and events. In Saskatchewan, the same is true of the Liquor and Gaming Authority, which also licenses charitable organisations and events. An added complication in the province is the additional level of participation provided by the Saskatchewan Indian Gaming Authority, which operates slot machines in half a dozen casinos. Yet these are owned and managed by the provincial authority, which manages video lottery terminals, and is the licensing agent for most gambling activities. It also registers all provincial gaming employees and gaming suppliers. Finally, Manitoba's Liquor and Gaming Authority is now that province's regulator and licenser of all gaming products – responsibilities once shared between governmental agencies, but now centralised.

The Western province not covered by the corporation is British Columbia, where the Gaming Policy and Enforcement Branch of the Ministry of Finance licenses and regulates lotteries, casinos, electronic gaming, and charitable organisations and events. However, as with Loto-Québec, lotteries and casinos in the province are operated by the British Columbia Lottery Corporation (BCLC). The two bodies are very similar, but BCLC is more active in contracting with the private sector than Loto-Québec.

Moving eastward, the Alcohol and Gaming Commission of Ontario regulates the charitable and commercial gaming sector, licences charitable organisations and events, and regulates the Ontario Lottery and Gaming Commission (OLG). The OLG, in turn, licenses lottery retailers, and operates casinos and other gaming activities (including electronic gaming) through contracts with private companies. OLG also provides electronic gaming products in Charitable Gaming Centres. This model appears to be as centralised as the Québec one; but Ontario's gaming operations are mainly contracted out to the private sector, while Loto-Québec manages and operates its activities directly. As noted above, in Québec there is very little involvement of the private sector.

All provincial governments interpret the term 'lottery' very loosely to include the sports-betting activities that operate within their borders (Campbell et al., 2005) – since, as indicated earlier, there are no national sports-betting lotteries in Canada. Both Lottery Corporations offer regional online sports-betting lotteries, based mainly on pools.

From this jurisdictional overview, we can see how the three regulatory approaches – Joint-Venture (JV), Charitable (Ch), and Government Ownership and Control (GOC) – apply to sports betting in Canada. An analysis of lotteries across the provinces reveals which of those approaches are most widely used. To sort the data, we divided the entities involved in gambling activities into four roles: regulator, licenser, operator and retailer. We also subdivided each type into commercial and charitable gambling, since these are always treated differently in Canada. We then listed all organisations involved in lotteries in each province, identifying the type and role of each – considering that an organisation might have more than one role. The resulting data set is listed below in Table 1.1.

This list allowed us to analyse how often each type of organisation assumed what kind of role in the provincial lottery sector. We treated departmental organisations, public corporations, regional corporations and governmental agencies as GOC; private contractors as JV; and charitable and religious organisations as Ch. We mapped each approach according to what province it was most prevalent in, as shown in Figure 1.1.

This analysis reveals four conclusions. First, there is no one specific approach. Although the frequency of involvement by private sector and charitable organisations differs from one province to another, it is evident that all have adopted a hybrid regulatory method. Second, despite some variations between provinces, the GOC approach is the

Table 1.1 Organisations involved in lotteries, by activities and province

Province	Organisation	Type of Organisation	Regulator Commercial	Regulator Charitable	Licenser Commercial	Licenser Charitable	Operator Commercial	Operator Charitable	Retailer Commercial	Retailer Charitable
Newfoundland and Labrador	Department of Public Safety	Departmental	X							
	Service Newfoundland & Labrador	Departmental		X						
	Atlantic Lottery Corporation	Regional Corporation			X		X			
	Charitable and Religious Events	Charitable						X		
	Private Contractors	Private							X	
Prince Edward Island	Department of Justice & Public Safety	Departmental		X		X				
	Lotteries Commissions	Public Corporation	X							
	Atlantic Lottery Corporation	Regional Corporation			X		X			
	Charitable and Religious Events	Charitable						X		
	Private Contractors	Private							X	
Nova Scotia	Alcohol and Gaming Division	Departmental	X	X	X	X	X			
	Atlantic Lottery Corporation	Regional Corporation					X			
	Charitable and Religious Events	Charitable						X		
	Private Contractors	Private							X	

(continued)

Table 1.1 (Cont.)

Province	Organisation	Type of Organisation	Regulator		Licenser		Operator		Retailer	
			Commercial	Charitable	Commercial	Charitable	Commercial	Charitable	Commercial	Charitable
New Brunswick	Gaming Control Branch	Departmental	X	X						
	Lotteries and Gaming Corporations	Public Corporation								
	Atlantic Lottery Corporation	Regional Corporation			X		X			
	Charitable and Religious Events	Charitable						X		
	Service Providers	Private							X	
Québec	Régie des alcools et des jeux	Governmental Agency	X	X	X	X				
	Loto-Québec	Public Corporation					X			
	Charitable and Religious Events	Charitable						X		X
	Private Contractors	Private							X	
Ontario	Alcohol and Gaming Commission	Governmental Agency	X	X		X				
	Ontario Lottery and Gaming Corporation	Public Corporation			X					
	Charitable and Religious Events	Charitable						X		
	Service Providers	Private					X		X	

Province	Organization	Type							
Manitoba	Liquor and Gaming Authority	Governmental Agency	x		x	x	x		
	Western Canada Lottery Corporation	Regional Corporation						x	
	Charitable and Religious Events	Charitable							x
	Private Contractors	Private							x
Saskatchewan	Saskatchewan Liquor and Gaming Authority	Governmental Agency	x		x	x	x		
	Saskatchewan Lotteries	Charitable						x	
	Western Canada Lottery Corporation	Regional Corporation						x	
	Private Contractors	Private							x
Alberta	Alberta Gaming Liquor Commission	Governmental Agency	x		x	x	x		
	Western Canada Lottery Corporation	Regional Corporation						x	
	Charitable and Religious Events	Charitable							x
	Private Contractors	Private							x
British Columbia	Gaming Policy and Enforcement Branch	Departmental	x		x	x	x		
	British Columbia Lottery Corporation	Public Corporation						x	
	Charitable and Religious Events	Charitable						x	
	Private Contractors	Private							x

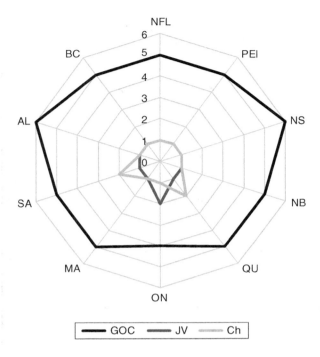

Figure 1.1 Major approaches in provincial lottery regulations

most dominant across the country. Third, Ontario has the strongest presence of the JV approach. This is no surprise, since Ontario's casinos were almost entirely developed as joint ventures. Fourth, the charitable approach (Ch) is most popular in Saskatchewan and Québec. This was unexpected, since we had assumed (based on a review of the literature) that the involvement of charitable organisations would be strongest in Alberta.

The coherence of the regulations

Given that Canada's legal attitude to sports betting is inconsistent across the provinces, we might reasonably address the question of just how fragmented the framework is. To answer this question, we used a relational-based approach to measure coherence (Savard, 2015). This seems a relevant issue, given that the negative impacts of a *lack* of coherence may include many adverse social and legal consequences to Canadian society. These range from preventing proper implementation of sports betting, and undermining public trust in provincial governments, to tax avoidance and money laundering by criminal elements (Azoulay, 2005; Hoebink, 2001; Koschinsky & Swanstrom, 2001; Piccioto, 2005). As a result, assessing the extent of coherence or fragmentation can identify any specific incoherent areas that are more sensitive to negative impacts.

The relational-based approach uses a three-step method. The first step analyses the information provided, to identify which related elements should be compared with one another. The second step assembles pairs of elements that we characterise as either coherent or incoherent. If a pair is deemed coherent, we assign it a value of 1; if incoherent, we assign it a value of -1. (A value of 0 indicates that pair elements are neither coherent nor incoherent; however, we included no independent relations with a value of 0.) Once all elements of a set are assigned a value, we measure its coherence using the Policy Coherence Index (PCI) software.[2] The third step uses the index data to create graphical representations of the coherence calculated, allowing us to identify specific incoherent zones.

In our analysis, we first used the data from Table 1.1 to identify all the provincial agencies and organisations that shape the lottery framework. We did not include operators, since their role is merely to implement the games; but we did include licensers, since theirs is part of the regulating role. Several agencies assume both roles, and we differentiated between them. To obtain more detailed results, we also considered commercial and charitable lotteries separately.

To perform the analysis, we identified the elements, assembled them in pairs, and characterised their relationship based on our observation of their coherence (1) or incoherence (-1). We used the PCI software to separately measure the coherence indexes of commercial and charitable lottery *regulation*, and also of commercial and charitable lottery *licensing*. The results were striking: the commercial lottery licensing framework had a negative PCI of -0.45 – a strong incoherent index. The two other frameworks had a positive PCI of 0.169, which only shows a very mild coherence. Taken together, their total PCI value was -0.052 – which is a mild incoherence. These results confirm how the literature qualified the gambling regulatory framework across the Canadian provinces: as fragmented and inconsistent.

Having established numerically the extent of incoherence, we turn to the relational structure graphs created by our software. As illustrated in Figures 1.2 to 1.6, all the graphs show clear zones of incoherence. Although the inconsistencies vary from one province and regulatory framework to another, some patterns emerge. It seems, for instance, that a handful of organisations have a huge negative impact on the

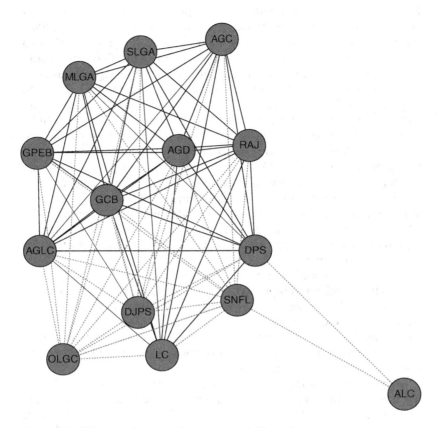

Figure 1.2 Coherence in regulating commercial lotteries
See Appendix A for matching code and organisations.

coherence of the whole. These organisations include Newfoundland's Department of Public Safety; Service Newfoundland; Prince Edward Island's Department of Justice and Public Safety, and its Lotteries Commissions; and Ontario's Lottery and Gaming Corporation. To confirm this observation of coherence and incoherence zones, we measured the positive or negative impact of each organisation for each relational structure, as shown in Table 1.2. The impact measure confirmed our first assessment based on the relational structure graphics.

Our analysis of the regulatory framework for sports betting in Canada reveals that the main extent of the fragmentation and inconsistency is in three provinces: Newfoundland and Labrador, Prince Edward Island, and Ontario. The rest of the provinces contribute positively to

Canada's regulatory framework for sports betting 19

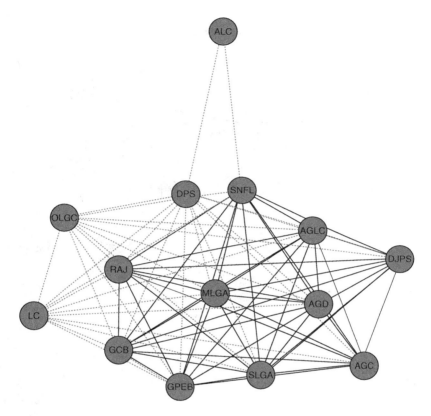

Figure 1.3 Coherence in regulating charitable lotteries

coherence – though as indicated earlier, and shown in Table 1.2, the positive effect is mild at best. Overall, the system is still very sensitive to negative impacts. This result suggests that there is a lot of room for improvement in terms of regulating sports betting. The inconsistencies could, for instance, prove to be loopholes that criminals could exploit for activities such as money laundering or tax avoidance. More research is clearly needed on this matter.

Another aspect to consider is that the lack of legal sports-betting activities in Canada logically leads to a black market, as Canadian gamblers look to find other outlets. It is no secret that Canada, like the United States, struggles with illegal book-making. And the modern increase in internet gambling has also given rise to a 'grey market' (Kelley, Todosichuk & Azmier, 2001). Many sports-betting websites are hosted in

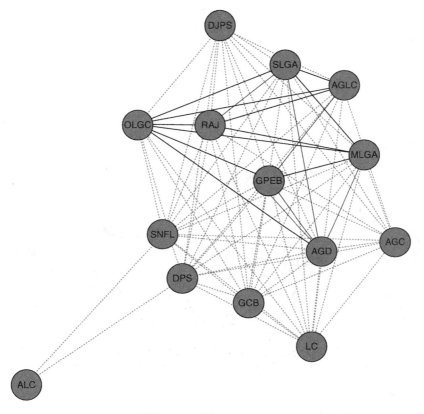

Figure 1.4 Coherence in licensing commercial lotteries

other countries, where they are legal; and so Canada has no authority over either the foreign websites, or the Canadians who gamble there (Deber, Gamble & Mah, 2010). As well, nothing prevents Canadians from crossing the border to the United States and gambling on sport events in places where it is legal, such as in Nevada. This can be viewed as an economic problem for Canada, since money spent in the United States disappears from this country's coffers. If sports-betting services were legal in Canada, that money could fund our own public revenues.

What's next?

Our consideration of the Canadian regulatory framework for gambling shows how greatly it has evolved over the last 124 years, since 1892. Nor

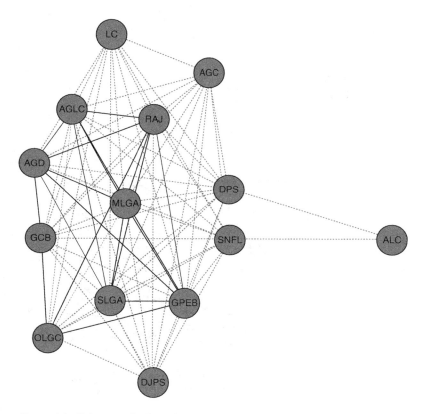

Figure 1.5 Coherence in licensing charitable lotteries

has this evolution necessarily halted in the present day. In November 2011, Joe Comartin, an NDP Member of Parliament for Windsor, Ontario, introduced a private member's bill to repeal paragraph 207(4) of the Criminal Code. If passed, the bill would legalise single-event sports betting – and open a new chapter for gambling in Canada. It would enable the provinces to remove sports betting from the lotteries category, and open it up to a whole new market.

What's interesting about this proposed amendment is the reasons put forward to support it. The MPs and senators who promoted the bill argue that it would help to better control gambling activities in Canada, and combat illegal betting and criminal activities. But the main reasons are economic, exactly as in 1969 and 1985. Ideally the move would help to create new jobs; bring new money into the Canadian economy; and

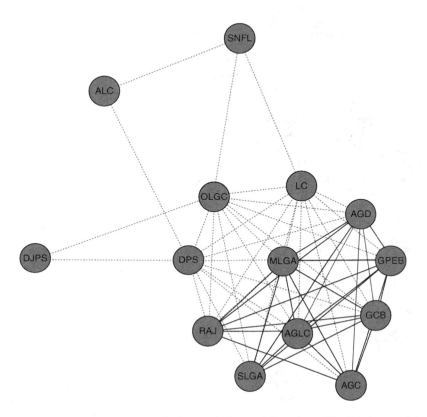

Figure 1.6 Coherence in both the regulating and licensing of both commercial and charitable lotteries

keep at home gambling money that might otherwise be spent in Nevada. For these reasons – again, just like 1969 and 1985 – the provinces have pressured the federal government to pass the bill.

But so far, they have been unsuccessful. Bill C-290 unanimously passed its first reading in the House of Commons in March 2012, and was sent on to the Senate. It has languished there ever since. The bill died on the Order Paper in September 2013, but was reinstated in October 2013. However, it died once again in August 2015, when the House of Commons rose for the election that year. So the bill remains in limbo, unable to come into force until it passes its Senate reading and receives Royal Assent.[3]

This situation is an unusual one, since the Canadian Senate (being unelected) usually passes bills it receives from the House of Commons

Table 1.2 Coherence index of organisations

		Commercial Lottery Regulation	Charitable Lottery Regulation	Commercial Lottery Licensing	Charitable Lottery Licensing	Regulation and Licensing of All Lotteries
Newfoundland and Labrador	DPS	6	−12	−12	−12	−7.5
	SNFL	−12	6	−12	6	−3
Prince Edward Island	DJPS	−11	7	−11	7	−2
	LC	7	−11	−11	−11	−6.5
Nova Scotia	AGD	6	6	0	6	4.5
New Brunswick	GCB	6	6	−12	6	1.5
Atlantic	ALC	−2	−2	−2	−2	−2
Québec	RAJ	6	6	0	6	4.5
Ontario	AGC	7	7	−11	7	2.5
	OLGC	−11	−11	1	−11	−8
Manitoba	MLGA	6	6	0	6	4.5
Saskatchewan	SLGA	6	6	0	6	4.5
Alberta	AGLC	6	6	0	6	4.5
British Columbia	GPEB	6	6	0	6	4.5

almost automatically. Its opposition to the proposed bill seems not to be based on its actual contents. During discussions in the Senate, questions were asked on a number of aspects. Would provinces be able to opt out of the sports-betting programme? (Answer: yes.) Would interprovincial sports betting be allowed? (Yes, since interprovincial gambling is already legal.) What would be the effect on revenue opportunities for First Nations? (None, since the bill would not change the current situation.) To what use would the new revenues generated by sport bets be put? (That was not yet decided; but the Criminal Code has never determined the use of funding.) It is possible that opposition to the bill is entirely political. Some senators felt that they had not had a chance to express their concerns, and asked that the bill be more extensively debated. Others might wish to use the issue of gambling (which, like drug legalisation, is a hot-button topic) to strategically strengthen their position within the Senate. It is also true that in Canada, private bills are very rarely enacted into law.

Regardless of the real reason, the fact remains that single-event sports betting remains illegal in Canada. However, the mere existence of Bill C-290 is a good indication that the issue is important enough to probably be raised again – at a time when it might stand a better chance of being passed by the Senate. After all, the Canadian economy is still fragile, and the provinces have a hard time balancing their budgets without raising taxes. As Joe Comartin has pointed out, gambling is worth some $450 million a year across the nation. New revenues from sports betting would be more than welcome.

Appendix A Organisations' Code by Province

Code	Province	Organisation
AGC	Ontario	Alcohol and Gaming Commission
AGD	Nova Scotia	Alcohol and Gaming Division
AGLC	Alberta	Alberta Gaming Liquor Commission
ALC	Newfoundland and Labrador	Atlantic Lottery Corporation
DJPS	Prince Edward Island	Department of Justice & Public Safety
DPS	Newfoundland and Labrador	Department of Public Safety
GCB	New Brunswick	Gaming Control Branch
GPEB	British Columbia	Gaming Policy and Enforcement Branch
LC	Prince Edward Island	Lotteries Commission
MLGA	Manitoba	Manitoba Liquor and Gaming Authority
OLGC	Ontario	Ontario Lottery and Gaming Corporation
RAJ	Québec	Régie des alcools et des jeux
SLGA	Saskatchewan	Saskatchewan Liquor and Gaming Authority
SNFL	Newfoundland and Labrador	Service Newfoundland & Labrador

Notes

1 Unlike most democratic countries, Canada's constitution is both unwritten and written. It is largely based on the example of the United Kingdom, where the constitution is partly based on unwritten conventions and jurisprudence. However, the written part of Canada's own constitution is made up of four different acts: the Royal Proclamation of 1791; the Constitutional Act of 1867 (which divides power between federal and provincial governments); the Westminster Statute of 1935 (which provides Canada with international sovereignty); and the Constitutional Act of 1982.
2 This software is a tool developed by a joint team of researchers from the School of Public Administration of Université du Québec, and the Swiss Graduate School of Public Administration (Institut des hautes études en administration publique). The PCI is easy to read: a value of 1 indicates a perfect coherence, and a value of -1 a perfect incoherence. The closer the PCI is to one, the stronger the coherence; and the closer it is to -1, the stronger the incoherence.
3 Comartin, who has since retired from public office, calls the Senate's stalling of the bill 'shameful'. He was formerly a member of the Standing Committee on Justice and Human Rights, which in 2012 prepared a report on organised crime in Canada. Of his bill, Comartin said: 'It's a great way to fight organized crime ... a great tool to take away a huge chunk of money from that type of activity.'

References

Azmier, J. J. (2005). *Gambling in Canada 2005: Statistics and Context*. Vancouver: Canada West Foundation.
Azmier, J. J., Jepson, V. & Patton, S. (1999). *Canada's Gambling Regulatory Patchwork: A Handbook*. Vancouver: Canada West Foundation.
Azmier, J. J. & Smith, G. (1998). *The State of Gambling in Canada: An Interprovincial Roadmap of Gambling and its Impact*. Vancouver: Canada West Foundation.
Azoulay, G. (2005). Cohérence des politiques commerciales et sécurité alimentaire. *European Journal of Development Research*, 17(3), 545–558. http://doi.org/10.1080/09578810500209809
Black, E. (1996). Gambling mania: Lessons from the Manitoba experience. *Canadian Public Administration/Administration Publique Du Canada*, 39(1), 49–61.
Bowal, P. & Carrasco, C. (1997). Taking a chance on it: The legal regulation of gambling. *Law Now*, 22(2), 28–33. http://doi.org/10.1017/CBO9781107415324.004
Burgess, M. (1993). Federalism and Federation: A Reappraisal. In M. Burgess & A. G. Gagnon (Eds.), *Comparative Federalism and Federation: Competing Traditions and Future Decision*. Toronto: University of Toronto Press.
Campbell, C. S., Hartnagel, T. F. & Smith, G. J. (2005). *La légalisation du jeu au Canada* Ottawa: Commission du droit du Canada.

Campbell, C. S. & Smith, G. J. (2003). Gambling in Canada, from vice to disease to responsibility: A negotiated history. *Canadian Bulletin of Medical History/ Bulletin Canadien D'histoire de La Médecine, 20*(1), 121–49. Retrieved from www.ncbi.nlm.nih.gov/pubmed/13678046

Campbell, C. S. & Smith, G. J. (1998). Canadian gambling: Trends and public policy issues. *American Academy of Political and Social Science, 556*, 22–35.

Canada Criminal Code, C-46 Minister of Justice 1131 (2015). Ottawa. Retrieved from http://laws-lois.justice.gc.ca/PDF/C-46.pdf

Deber, R. B., Gamble, B. & Mah, C. L. (2010). Canada: Variations on a common theme. *Italian Journal of Public Health, 7*(4), 336–343. Retrieved from www.scopus.com/inward/record.url?eid=2-s2.0-79956294161&partnerID=40&md5=ec63273e0601bd6f9946b116e10410b9

Gibbins, R. (1987). *Federalism and the Role of the State*. Toronto: University of Toronto Press.

Hoebink, P. (2001). *Evaluating Maastricht's Triple C: The 'C' of Coherence*. Brussels: European Union.

Kelley, R., Todosichuk, P. & Azmier, J. J. (2001). *GAMBLING@HOME: Internet Gambling in Canada*. Vancouver: Canada West Foundation.

Koschinsky, J. & Swanstrom, T. (2001). Confronting policy fragmentation: A political approach to the role of housing nonprofits. *Policy Studies Review, 18*(4), 111–127.

McRoberts, K. (1993). Federal Structures and the Policy Process. In M. Atkinson (Ed.), *Governing Canada: Institution and Public Policy*. Toronto: Harcourt Brace Jovanovich.

Osborne, J. A. (1989). *The Legal Status of Lottery Schemes in Canada: Changing the Rules of the Game*. Vancouver: Faculty of Law, University of British.

Osborne, J. A. & Campbell, C. S. (1988). Recent amendments to Canadian lottery and gaming laws: The transfer of power between federal and provincial governments. *Osgoode Hall Law Journal, 26*(1), 19–43.

Piccioto, R. (2005). The evaluation of policy coherence for development. *Evaluation 11*(3), 311–330.

Savard, J.-F. (2015). *La mesure de la cohérence des politiques publiques: Fondements et proposition d'une méthode*. Lausanne: Institut des hautes études en administration publique (Working Paper, IDHEAP No. 4/2015).

Watts, R. (1998). *Comparaison des régimes fédéraux des années 1990*. Kingston: Institut des relations intergouvernementales.

2 Multidimensional performance of sports betting operators

Lea Meyer

Balancing the parallel needs of shareholders and customers, as well as third party requirements, is a fundamental operational challenge for sports betting organisations. Indeed, the specific regulatory framework in which they are placed imposes obligations in regard to economic, legal, social and environmental matters. At the same time, consumers are increasingly aware of the manner in which organisations conduct their business. Directing organisations successfully entails a management focus that is not limited to financial and operational performance, but must also include evaluating performance in social issues. Recent betting fraud scandals, problems of gambling addiction, the risks of money laundering, and calls for organisations to have a positive social impact make the need for balancing financial, operational, legal and social objectives in the sports betting sector incontrovertible.

This chapter aims to offer an instrument to conceptualise multidimensional performance and discuss the need for a multidimensional performance strategy for sports betting organisations. Such a strategy allows organisations in general, and sports betting operators specifically, to offer a more sophisticated and meaningful view of performance to the spectrum of stakeholders. This in turn can lead to new opportunities for growth and value creation. Much more importantly, it can help organisations reframe their relationship with the regulator and win greater support from the society in which they are embedded.

The regulatory environment has a huge influence on how sports betting organisations define their performance. As a consequence, gambling operators face the challenge of balancing the pursuit of increasing shareholder value with the social impacts created by offering games of chance. A question arising from this balancing act is whether social activities (such as responsible gambling) are actually embedded in the strategy of sports betting organisations and subject to measurement. Before discussing the need for a balanced, multidimensional performance definition, the motivation of gambling regulation will be presented, as this goes some way in making the case for the need to take into account non-economic aspects when thinking about performance. Further, a framework to evaluate the regulatory intensity of a specific sector is presented as this and the specific components have to be addressed by organisations in their performance strategy.

Rationale for gambling regulation

Sports betting is, in most countries, a regulated activity (Anderson et al., 2012). The motivations behind regulation are very similar from one country to another. Firstly there is the economic benefit of games of chance. Statistics show that the gambling 'industry' – encompassing all its sectors – generates substantial revenues. In 2008, the GGR of the gambling market in the EU was estimated at 75.9 billion Euros. The online gambling market share of this was 6.16 billion Euros (European Commission, 2011). States clearly have an economic interest in keeping a share of the revenues generated by games of chance. This can be done either through taxes or through the exploitation of games of chance by public enterprises (Littler, 2008; Littler et al., 2011).

Next to this economic interest, *security issues* provide a second rationale for gambling regulation. Organised crime has penetrated some gambling markets by way of money laundering, fraud and corruption. The betting scandals in the football world are only the most recent examples of such criminal conduct. Money laundering has found an ideal setting in gambling 'because of its big volumes and frequent transactions' (Viren, 2008: p. 10). Indeed, '[l]aw enforcement representatives [have] said that the anonymity and jurisdictional issues characteristic of Internet gambling make online gaming a potentially powerful tool for money launderers. They noted that few money laundering cases involving Internet gambling had been prosecuted but attributed the small number of cases primarily to a lack of regulation and oversight' (United States General Accounting Office, 2002: 2). These legal challenges require adaptations to regulatory frameworks and the proper allocation of resources.

Another criminal activity that calls for gambling regulation is illegal gambling, both land-based (in back-stores) and cross-border (via internet). Though illegal gambling is very hard to quantify, it clearly represents a worldwide phenomenon, and online illegal gambling in particular is spreading. Illegal gambling includes lotteries, betting and casino games. In Switzerland, illegal online gambling generated a GGR of around 1 to 2 million Swiss francs (CHF) for the operators via lottery games, 34 million CHF via sports betting and 39 million CHF via casino games in 2007. Around 35,000 people play illegal lotteries and betting games online in Switzerland, and around 40,000 play illegal casino games (Fachdirektorenkonferenz Lotteriemarkt und Lotteriegesetz, 2009). The illegal operators can be categorised into two groups. The first group is made up of so-called 'grey market' operators, who are licensed in one country but who offer games of chance online illegally in other. Most of those operators hold a valid licence in a country allowing online gambling such as Malta, Gibraltar or the Isle of Man, but they do not respect the national borders in their activities. Next to these grey market operators, there are the so-called 'black market' operators, who do not hold a licence in any nation state. The problem with illegal operators is that they do not comply with obligations imposed on legal operators, such as taxation or prevention measures. Thus the social and economic costs are left to be dealt with by the target countries.

The fourth reason to regulate games of chance is problem gambling. This negative external effect is characterised by enduring and repeated dysfunctional gambling behaviour that diminishes personal, familiar or professional aims. As well as financial and psychological issues, problem gambling can have a negative impact on players' relatives (e.g. loss of employment, divorce, debts) and for society more generally. Gambling addiction is a problem for the persons afflicted by it, but is also an issue in terms of the limitations it puts on the operations of organisers. In a sense, it threatens the business model by introducing limitations and blockages at the social and political levels. Organisers are obliged to face this challenge, as are political authorities, for both political and social reasons. Hence, gambling addiction can constitute another rationale for gambling regulation. It is common for regulations to force operators to take measures to limit or prevent addiction. Operators can be obliged to monitor or inform gamblers, or implement bans blocking the access of certain gamblers to the premises (mostly for casinos). Another rationale for gambling regulation is the protection of minors. In most jurisdictions, minors cannot participate in gambling activities and the regulation requires operators to ensure that minors have no access to gambling.

States generally establish gambling regulations for one or several of these rationales. In so doing, they need to balance economic objectives with social ones. In most systems, the government collects a part or the total of the benefits. The use of the extra income varies: some cover state deficits, others accomplish public tasks, and others still use the money to support benevolent or charitable projects. Obviously, they face a paradoxical situation: having to weigh the economic benefits generated through the games of chance against the risks in terms of criminality and addiction. This trade-off is reflected in most gambling regulations. The UK Gambling Act 2005, for example, clearly states in its very first section that the objectives of licensing are, *inter alia*, to prevent gambling from being a source or a tool for crime and to ensure that it is conducted in a fair and open manner, protecting children and vulnerable persons (United Kingdom, 2005).

However, while the regulation of gambling is a universal phenomenon, and while such regulation tends to share the same motivations and components across countries, regulation does differ in terms of its intensity. The regulatory intensity can be evaluated based on different parameters (Meyer, 2015), which can be grouped into two main dimensions: regulatory scope and regulatory stringency (e.g. Cook et al., 1983; Reger et al., 1992). In the next section we will briefly outline the different parameters.[1] This is important, as these parameters influence the operation environment of sports betting operators.

The first component defines to what extent the regulation affects a specific sector and organisation. This is called the regulatory scope and includes factors such as the market structure, i.e. the level of competition allowed in the sector, the regulatory reach, questioning whether there are further legal obligations beyond simply obtaining a license, the imposition of a specific public use of the net profits, the imposition of the type of ownership by the regulation or the presence of a public nature in the organisation, above and beyond the issue of ownership ('Publicness').

So collectively, these five factors constitute regulatory scope, which is one half of regulatory intensity. The second dimension is regulatory stringency. In contrast to the regulatory scope, which accounts for how much of the organisation is affected by the regulation, stringency is the degree to which the organisation's activities are constrained by regulation. It occurs on two levels – the regulator and the organisational level.

The level of the regulator focuses on whether there is actually a regulator or not, and if so, what are its competencies. This might seem simplistic but if nobody actually monitors the implementation of regulation or the body responsible for the implementation has no actual power, the regulation is not effective and will result in a low regulatory stringency. Also this looks at the level of professionalism of the regulator and investigates the sector-specific knowledge a regulator has or is acquiring.

Level of the organisation is the second dimension within stringency, and focuses on how regulation impacts the organisation's daily business. So this includes things like distribution channel restrictions, product and technical restrictions, advertisement restrictions and the legal obligation of internalising negative externalities. Gambling addiction, money laundering and other criminal activities are a feature of the industry and can be described as negative externalities. Internalisation investigates whether the regulation imposes a duty to take into account these externalities and minimise them.

Based on these parameters the regulatory intensity is evaluated. For example, in the Belgian sports betting sector numerous competitors are permitted, having only few restrictions for business operations. Similarly, sports betting in Austria is not a game of chance but a game of skill and hence no specific gambling regulation is in place. These are two examples where the intensity of the regulation is low. In contrast, the regulatory system of sports betting and lottery games in Norway can be described as of high regulatory intensity, as it limits operation to one public organisation, Norsk Tipping, and imposes several restrictions concerning distribution of products, products themselves and advertising.

This model provides a much more useful and applicable understanding of how regulation affects differing aspects of a business than traditional approaches, which do not offer the granularity of a management approach to regulation. When reflecting on regulation it is important to adopt a global perspective taking all aspects into account and not reduce it to fiscal and jurisdictional components.

Armed with this deeper analysis, organisations have the power to show regulators how their organisation is affected in multiple ways and how they respond to these influences while operating their business.

The call for a multidimensional performance strategy

Organisations need to interact with their environment and to adapt their structures to the external context if they want to survive and succeed. In regulated environments, where the opportunity to offer games of chance depends on the government allowing or giving the licence to one, few or many operators – depending upon the regulation in place – organisations are obliged to consider their environment in which they are operating. Failure to respect the regulation can endanger the organisation itself. Hence, it is crucial that they not only consider and manage their relationship with the regulator but also take serious account of the negative effects their business operations create.

Across countries, sports betting operators share the need to balance their objectives between the demands of the regulatory framework and the goals of economic efficiency. Voluntarily integrated, non-financial, social performance measures strengthen the position of a sports betting operator with regard to its regulator. Further, there is a greater need for organisations to perform in social and ecological dimensions as consumers and society are increasingly considering not only the quality of the products and price efficiency but also the way organisations produce and deliver the products and whether the organisation itself is a 'good citizen'.

There is an increasing awareness among both consumers and society in general about how operators conduct their business. This should shift the focus of managers from financial and organisational performance to other activities that broaden the performance definition. Performance is the instrument used to measure the level of an organisation's success. The factors an organisation include in its definition of success depends very much on its vision, mission and strategy. With strategic objectives, strategy is translated into practices and guides organisational activities. In order to evaluate whether strategic objectives are being achieved, and to identify the areas of success, an organisation establishes performance indicators.

Traditionally, the financial dimension has been the main performance focus. However, a spectrum of performance dimensions exist. In this chapter an argument is made for a multidimensional performance definition embracing six dimensions.

- The financial dimension, as the traditional performance criterion, refers to revenue and profits.
- The operational dimension focuses on how an organisation produces and delivers a service or product. It relates to internal processes and includes customer-related indicators, learning and growth indicators, and internal business processes indicators.
- Stakeholder management is the third dimension and it essentially looks at how well an organisation is doing with investors, employees and suppliers, i.e. actors who have, in one form or another, invested in the company.
- The fourth dimension is the legal requirement dimension. Here activities undertaken which are in compliance with regulatory obligations are measured.
- Social issue participation is the fifth dimension. It is not directly linked to shareholder value creation but rather it relates to activities that benefit wider society. The idea behind this is that companies should not only optimise short-term financial performance but also voluntarily create value in and for society (Carter and Greer, 2013).

- Sixth is the public values dimension which analyses performance of the values an organisation upholds – fairness, transparency, equality and inclusiveness.

So, we can see that performance is a construct based on different dimensions, measured by various indicators. Those indicators can be of a quantifiable or non-quantifiable, monetary or non-monetary, nature.

Ideally, performance in all dimensions should be evaluated based on pre-formulated targets that are measured through key performance indicators (Behn, 2003; Kaplan and Norton, 2008; Kaplan and Norton, 1996b; Kaplan and Norton, 1992; Kaplan and Norton, 1996a). Only if organisations have a clear idea about what they want to measure and how, can they determine their performance targets and decide upon a meaningful and sophisticated strategy to reach that target (Mintzberg, 2008; Boyne 2002b; Talbot, 2010).

Over recent years, especially with regard to concepts such as corporate social responsibility and corporate social performance, performance of non-financial activities is increasingly subject to measurement (Summermatter and Siegel, 2008; Basu and Palazzo, 2008; Palazzo and Richter, 2005; Talbot, 1998; Behn, 1998; Ittner and Larcker, 2003; Amirkhanyan et al., 2013). It is therefore an interesting question whether sports betting organisations apply a multidimensional performance by integrating social, ethical or legal aspects next to financial and operational considerations. For the sports betting industry this is doubly useful as it is regulated and under public scrutiny. This begs the question whether social activities are actually an integral part of the strategy of sports betting organisations and subject of measurement.

To evaluate this question, the performance definition has to be examined. At first sight the argument could be made that performance and responsible gambling are two sides of the same coin. Therefore, it could be that effective organisational performance requires and mandates an organisational engagement in social initiatives. For example, one could envisage a situation in which higher benefits would be problematic; a case where too many 'side effects' of gambling in the form of gambling addiction were to appear. Therefore, for the sports betting sector, and possibly also for any other similarly regulated sector, social responsibility would be the process through which actors manage to respect the non-formalised boundaries inherent in the spirit (as opposed to in the letter) of the social regulatory obligations, be it to ensure their short-term business survival and/or their long-term societal fit.

Is responsible gambling part of the performance definition?

With responsible gambling, sports betting operators want to ensure a fair and safe gaming environment that protects players from the negative consequences of gambling. At present nearly all (increasingly also the illegal ones) operators are referring to the concept of responsible gambling or responsible gaming. With responsible gambling, the organisations aim to address the different challenges the gambling activities have. However, what those challenges are exactly and which aspects organisations integrate in the notion of responsible gambling may differ significantly. Whether they then also measure the performance of their activities is a second important question. In order to give indications of how operators address the integrity challenges, we have to look at the definition of responsible gambling.

In the sports betting market, various definitions of responsible gambling exist. In order to have an idea of what responsible gambling refers to, we will look at the definition of the concept in two different organisations:[2] Ladbrokes in Belgium and Norsk Tipping, the Norwegian operator. These two organisations face different regulatory intensities, as illustrated above.

Ladbrokes in Belgium[3] includes several pillars in its concept of responsible gambling, engaging in measures to reduce addiction and diminish excessive risk. Among the measures are: staff training and information about gambling addiction, provision of information to players about responsible gambling, self-exclusion procedures, a partnership with a hospital to assist customers facing gambling addiction and responsible advertising. However, Ladbrokes' concept of responsible gambling places the onus heavily on the consumer and how far they wish to restrict their gambling behaviour. There are no mandatory measures taken by the organisations and no controls are established. This is also underlined in the responsible gaming policy of Ladbrokes that outlines principles for online gambling customers. Customers are *advised* to set a maximum loss limit, for a specific time, and to stick to that limit. They *should* never play to win at all costs but to remember that gambling is a pleasure. Further, customers *should* never borrow money to gamble and not use the money meant for important expenses. They *should* take regular breaks, alternate gambling with other activities, never play in period of stress, depression or confusion and remember that gambling is not to escape from the everyday problems. Thus Ladbrokes Belgium advises its customers to take these precautions, but does not control or actively offer help. Ladbrokes Belgium addresses with responsible gaming aspects that are legally required from the organisation. This is also illustrated by the second theme of their responsible gambling policy – minor/child protection.

Belgian law forbids minors (under 18) to bet online. Ladbrokes can ask at any moment the age of the customers. Further, they outline recommendations for parents in order to protect their children, such as setting up access blocking filters for online gambling websites, and explain gambling law and the danger of gambling addiction. Again, there are no automatic controls in place, and measures are only taken when under-age activity is suspected and the recommendations externalise the responsibility to a third party. Hence the concept of responsible gaming is one that devolves the responsibility to the players. Measures are reactive and the challenge of dysfunctional gambling activity is only internalised when the law makes it mandatory to do so.

Other organisations have a more proactive approach towards responsible gambling. Norsk Tipping,[4] the Norwegian lottery and betting operator, for example, includes in its concept of responsible gambling, several mandatory measures for customers. In order to be able to play, customers need to register and have a player card. This card provides Norsk Tipping with information on who, when, where, how and how much a customer gambles. Further, Norsk Tipping has implemented limit-setting systems and monitors the addictive potential of games. Staff and retail partners training is regularly organised and it also monitors gambling behaviour and develop in collaboration with problem gambling agencies measures to reduce risk behaviour. Moreover, it funds research in the area of responsible gambling. Norsk Tipping introduced an age limit of 18 years for all games. In addition to mandatory measures for customers, it can further set voluntary limits for stakes in all general games. Thus we can see that the responsible gambling policy of Norsk Tipping introduces mandatory measures on the players and the operations of games of chance. Further, it establishes measures that surpass that which is mandated by gambling regulation.

These two examples illustrate the differences in responsible gambling concepts that exist based on the degree to which the organisation shares that responsibility with its customers and the constraints imposed on games of chance by the regulatory framework. In the case of Ladbrokes in Belgium most of the measures contained in the notion of responsible gaming are voluntary and the instruments at the client's disposal are entirely the responsibility of the players, with the exception of minimum legal requirements. In the case of Norsk Tipping, the notion of responsible gambling includes both mandatory and voluntary measures for the customers and the organisation itself. Norsk Tipping is active in assisting and advising clients and does not rely entirely on their self-empowerment. The degree of implementation of responsible gambling in an organisation's strategic objectives can thus vary widely and it does not automatically follow that the achievements are measured or monitored along the lines of a multi-dimensional performance. In the case of Ladbrokes Belgium, in the annual report of 2011, not one statement of performance or a performance indicator is established for social or ethical matters. Norsk Tipping, on the other hand, developed several measures to evaluate the performance of responsible gambling.

Certainly, there are many other examples going in one or the other direction. The above discussion illustrates that the concept of responsible gambling has found a place in sports betting organisations' concept of operations, even though it is implemented differently. In order to unify the concept of responsibility in sports betting and to evaluate the level of organisational commitment to address this challenge, a key development is the establishment of certification systems. However, it is still an open question whether they contribute to a greater focus on social targets in the performance strategies of sports betting operators. The following section will discuss the role of these certifications more extensively.

Certification systems to strengthen the multidimensional organisational performance?

Certifications are an instrument with which organisations can commit to responsible gambling. Two such certification systems, which are important for the lottery and sports betting sectors, are the European Lotteries (EL) Responsible Gaming Standard and the World Lottery Associations (WLA) Responsible Gaming Framework.

The EL concept of responsible gambling, first adopted in 2007, includes illegal gambling and related criminal activities and problem gambling. The EL Responsible Gaming Standard outlines ten key areas for a responsible gaming business. Organisations that have a minimum score of 75 per cent in each of the areas[5] qualify for certification. The certificate attests that responsible gaming is an integral part of daily business operations. In order to comply with the standard, members have to specify outputs that are measurable. In order to evaluate whether measures in the area of responsible gambling are meaningful or not, the key question is whether the performance in the activities taken in line with the responsible gaming or gambling is actually measured and monitored and in case of bad performance, if measures are taken to improve it.

The level of compliance with standards can vary significantly. This is illustrated with the seven WLA Responsible Gaming Principles,[6] which aim to foster public order, to fight against illegal gambling and to make responsible gaming an integral part of daily operations. With the Responsible Gaming Framework, organisations can certify their level of commitment to the principles. Four levels of achievement exist to mirror the level of compliance and commitment to responsible gambling practices. The first level consists of the commitment to the Responsible Gaming Framework. Organisations achieve this level by simple adherence to the WLA. The second level consists of self-assessment and has to determine responsible gambling programmes that address all the WLA responsible gaming principles. To achieve the third level organisations have to plan, schedule and budget the implementation of specific responsible gambling programmes. In the fourth level, organisations implement specific programmes in their daily operations and are continuously improving them. The specific programmes have to be in the areas of research, employee programmes, retailer programmes, game design, remote gaming channels, advertising and marketing communications, player education, treatment referral, stakeholder engagement, reporting and measurement.

It is only when reporting and measurement is outlined and responsible gambling is integrated into operations strategy, that organisations are certified at this level. Thus responsible gambling can span a low level, based on voluntarism and individual responsibility, to a high level of commitment where the different activities of responsible gambling are followed up. However, even with this framework, responsible gambling frequently does not enter the performance strategy of organisations. It is the view of the author that a level 5 should be introduced in which organisations outline measures and actions when they are underperforming in regard to responsible gambling. Further, in order to increase commitment, the effects of responsible gambling initiatives should be evaluated and the results could be used in an information and performance reporting cycle continuously improving the social issue participation standards of the organisation.

Discussion

Regulation imposes obligations on an organisation in regard to economic, legal, social, societal and environmental matters. Organisations have to respond to this by addressing the issues in their business operations. Today, the concept of responsible gambling is mainly used to highlight the organisation's commitment to address the negative externalities of the gambling business. However, the definition of responsible gambling varies among organisations. Some apply a definition complying with the legal obligations, whereas others go further by voluntarily restricting their businesses.

Both the definition of responsible gambling on the organisational level and the development of certification systems are important trends illustrating how organisations take into account the necessity to respond to negative effects of their operations. However, what an organisation puts under the concept of responsible gambling varies widely. Even more important is the question whether organisations measure the level of performance in non-financial activities and take actions in cases of underperformance, as would be done with financial and operational indicators. Only then are these aspects fully integrated in organisations' strategy and daily business operations. A performance strategy including the social issue participation dimension is not yet widely used as a measure of success. Only in level four of the WLA framework is a link to performance made. For individual organisations, there are some, as the example of Norsk Tipping has shown, measuring performance by the use of indicators for non-financial activities. Others, as in the case of Ladbrokes, have no multidimensional definition of performance. A multidimensional definition of performance is, however, very beneficial as a tool helping to outline how and to what extent they incorporate the challenges of conducting business in a sensitive sector such as sports betting.

In concluding this discussion, three areas are identified, where a multidimensional performance model is valuable to organisations and serves as a key structure in addressing the negative externalities of sports betting. Naturally, the product itself is very important but how the company makes and delivers its product to the marketplace and how it expresses its values can be the deciding factors when faced with two companies with a similar offering. With a multidimensional performance, organisations are empowered to show customers that they hold values beyond simply the bottom-line. Second, the use of multidimensional performance gives organisations a tool to anticipate possible areas of future regulation and allow them to take individual measures to prevent or shape further state regulation. An organisation able to demonstrate that it is at least as concerned as their regulator about their external impact is much more likely to have a voice in the formation and establishment of regulation. Finally, organisations operating in socially controversial areas have an interest in being as proactive as possible in the protection of their reputations. It is not enough to simply articulate core values. An organisation able to demonstrate that it both holds and measures the social responsibility is better able to safeguard its reputation.

Conclusion

This chapter has shown why sports betting is a regulated activity in most countries, and how organisations address the challenge of generating significant revenue while at the same time acting responsibly, i.e. considering social values and minimising negative externalities. Further, it has shown that there are developments on the level of organisations and associations to include and evaluate the responsibility of the operators. However, to what extent the negative externalities are taken as strategic objectives vary. Organisations rarely measure the performance of corporate social responsibility activities. However this is vital in judging whether corporate social responsibility is merely cosmetic or an important and genuine value the organisation holds. This calls for a multidimensional definition of performance – not only for sports betting operators but all organisations operating in sensitive environments.

Notes

1 For an extensive discussion please see the authors' previous publications such as Meyer 2015.
2 Document analysis of annual reports and main communications as well as information published on the website. Base year of the analysis is 2011/2012.
3 Information is retrieved from the website of Ladbrokes in Belgium: http://contact.ladbrokes.be/#/ (last accessed 28 July 2014).
4 Information is retrieved from the website of Norsk Tipping: www.norsk-tipping.no/ (last accessed 28 July 2014).
5 The areas are research, employee training, sales agents' programmes, game design, remote gaming channels, advertising and marketing, treatment referral, player education, stakeholder engagement, reporting, measurement and certification, Electronic Gaming Machines (EGMs).
6 World Lottery Association, www.world-lotteries.org/cms/index.php?option=com_content&view=article&id=3894&Itemid=100192&lang=en (last accessed 25 July 2014).

References

Amirkhanyan, A. A., Kim, H. J. & Lambright, K. T. (2013). The performance puzzle: understanding the factors influencing alternative dimensions and views of performance. *Journal of Public Administration Research and Theory*, 31.

Anderson, P. M., Blackshaw, I. S., Siekmann, R. C. R. & Soek, J. (eds.) (2012). *Sports Betting: Law and Policy*, The Hague: TMC Asser Press.
Basu, K. & Palazzo, G. (2008). Corporate social responsibility: a process model of sensemaking. *Academy of Management Review, 33*, 122–136.
Behn, R. D. (1998). The new public management paradigm and the search for democratic accountability. *International Public Management Journal, 1*, 131–164.
Behn, R. D. (2003). Why measure performance? Different purposes require different measures. *Public Administration Review, 63*, 586–606.
Boyne, G. A. (2002b). Concepts and indicators of local authority performance: an evaluation of the statutory frameworks in England and Wales. *Public Money and Management, 22*, 17–24.
Carter, S. M. & Greer, C. R. (2013). Strategic leadership: values, styles, and organizational performance. *Journal of Leadership & Organizational Studies.*
Cook, K., Shortell, S. M., Conrad, D. A. & Morrisey, M. A. (1983). A theory of organizational response to regulation: the case of hospitals. *The Academy of Management Review, 8*(2), 193. doi:10.2307/257746
European Commission (2011). Green paper on on-line gambling in the internal market. Brussels: EC.
Fachdirektorenkonferenz Lotteriemarkt und Lotteriegesetz (2009). Glücksspiel im Internet – Schlussbericht. Gerlafingen: FDKL.
Ittner, C. D. & Larcker, D. F. (2003). Coming up short on nonfinancial performance measurement. *Harvard Business Review, 81*, 88–95.
Kaplan, R. S. & Norton, D. P. (1992). The balanced scorecard – measures that drive performance. *Harvard Business Review*, 71, 69–79.
Kaplan, R. S. & Norton, D. P. (1996a). *The Balanced Scorecard.* Boston: Harvard Business School Press.
Kaplan, R. S. & Norton, D. P. (1996b). *The Balanced Scorecard: Translating Strategy into Action.* Cambridge, Mass.: Harvard Business School Press.
Kaplan, R. S. & Norton, D. P. (2008). *Le tableau de bord prospectif.* Paris: Eyrolles.
Littler, A. (2008). Regulatory perspectives on the future of interactive gambling in the internal market. *European Law Review*, 2.
Littler, A., Hoekx, N., Fijnaut, C. J. & Verbeke, A.-L. (eds.) (2011). *In the Shadow of Luxembourg: EU and National Developments in the Regulation of Gambling,* Leiden: Martinus Nijhoff.
Meyer, L. (2015). *The Influence of the Regulatory Environment on the Definition of Organisational Performance – The Example of the Sport Betting and Lottery Sectors.* Bern: Haupt Verlag.
Mintzberg, H., Ahlstrand, B. & Lampel, J. (2008). *Strategy Bites Back! It is Far More and Less Than You Have Ever Imagined.* London: FT Prentice Hall.
Palazzo, G. & Richter, U. (2005). CSR business as usual? The case of the tobacco industry. *Journal of Business Ethics,* 61, 387–401.
Summermatter, L. & Siegel, J. P. (2008). Defining performance in public management: a survey of academic journals. *European Group of Public Administration Conference.* Rotterdam.

Talbot, C. (1998). *Public Performance – Towards a Public Service excellence Model.* Llantilio Crossenny: Public Futures.

Talbot, C. (2010). *Theories of Performance: Organizational and Service Improvement in the Public Domain.* Oxford: Oxford University Press.

United Kingdom (2005). Gambling Act 2005. London.

United States General Accounting Office (2002). *Internet gambling: an overview of the issues.* Washington D.C.: GAO.

Viren, M. (2008). *Gaming in the New Market Environment.* Basingstoke: Palgrave Macmillan.

3 Cases of match-fixing in tennis and snooker

Dawn Aquilina

Introduction

Sport has ubiquitous appeal and consequently has propelled the sports industry to become a very powerful economic, political and social phenomenon. Mega-events such as the FIFA World Cup and the Olympic Games continue to attract billions of people, which in turn generates a number of lucrative deals in the shape of broadcasting rights packages, sponsorship deals, licensing of official merchandise and ticket sales, among others. For instance, in May 2014 the IOC awarded NBCUniversal the right to broadcast the Olympic Games in the United States across all media platforms, including free-to-air television, subscription television, internet and mobile. 'The agreement from 2021 to 2032 is valued at USD 7.65 billion, plus an additional USD 100 million signing bonus to be used for the promotion of Olympism and the Olympic values between 2015 and 2020' (IOC Press Release, May 2014).

Governments are major stakeholders in sports as they help to fund national and international sporting events. Historically, government funding has varied across sports and nations but it is widely accepted that if a country or governing sporting body wants to host an important sporting event, they must first secure government support before bidding. Governments are the guarantors for all major sport events, especially mega-events, which usually entail a significant amount of investment, for instance in building and/or renovating sporting infrastructure. It has been confirmed that the London Olympic Games in 2012 cost £9.3 billion (public funding figures released by NAO, 2012), which could not have taken place if the British government had not given its full support. As public interest in sport continues to increase and the financial stakes have equally risen, there has also been a growth in the inclination of major stakeholders 'to pursue legal claims requiring sport bodies to adopt effective risk management practices and insurance protocols to minimise legal and financial exposure' (EU Expert Group, 2013: p. 3).

With such high stakes surrounding sports, maintaining high levels of integrity and trust is of the essence. On a political level, the Council of Europe continues to be a firm believer in upholding the integrity of sport and has developed a Code of Sports Ethics that European Sport Ministers have agreed to promote (June 2010). More recently (2012) the Parliamentary Assembly has drafted a resolution on 'Good Governance and Ethics in Sport' that acknowledged the following:

> Sport plays an important role in personal development and social cohesion, as a powerful vehicle for the transmission of positive values and role models, particularly to young people. This role is closely linked to the respect and promotion, by all involved in the world of sport, of high ethical principles.

While recognising the widespread benefits of sport participation and competition, Chappelet and Theodoraki (2006) urged managers and policy-makers to promote and manage sport within an ethical framework in an attempt to pre-empt negative outcomes. However, following a period of unprecedented economic growth particularly through its increasing commercialisation as well as the rapid expansion of the global betting market, sport, particularly professional sport, became a fertile ground for corrupt behaviour. During the past decade alone, the integrity of sport has come under serious and persistent threat as a result of unregulated management misconduct, money laundering, corrupt betting, doping, tanking (athletes not giving their best effort during competition), espionage (illegal attainment of sensitive information), bribing and match-fixing.

Match-fixing has been heralded as one of the most serious threats to sport integrity by sport and political stakeholders, most notoriously the type that is orchestrated by illegal gambling syndicates. To date there has been a number of ways in which match-fixing has been defined in the literature, but in Europe policy makers and sport officials conferred on the following working definition: 'illegally influencing the course or the result of a sporting competition in order to obtain advantage for oneself or for others' (Brasseur, 2012: 6). Over the past decade, match-fixing has taken centre stage in the debates on corruption in sport since there has been a spate of European and international scandals that were uncovered in sports such as badminton, basketball, boxing, cricket, football, handball, rugby, tennis, snooker and sumo (Maennig, 2005; IRIS,

2012; Play the Game, 2014). As Maennig (2005) attested, although evidence of match-fixing in sport is not a recent development, the issue gained prominence as more cases exposing gambling corruption started to surface. This phenomenon has been further exacerbated 'with the rise of global, cross-border betting via the internet', affecting 'all sports from horse-racing and football, to cricket and snooker' (Transparency International, 2014).

Much of the attention by the mainstream media has targeted football as it enjoys public popularity and it attracts the greatest amount of money in betting than any other sport, making it an easy target for match-fixers. In a study on the prevalence of betting-related match-fixing in football, published by INTERPOL, it was estimated that more than 70 countries across six continents, were dealing with this issue from June 2012 to May 2013 (INTERPOL, 2013). On a similar note, FIFA declared that some 50 national leagues outside of Europe were being targeted by organised crime figures in the betting market and 'any country is vulnerable regardless of its record on corruption' (Reuters, 2013). Given these alarming statistics much of the academic attention has been directed towards football in an attempt to devise an effective integrity framework to deal with this crisis (Haberfeld & Sheehan, 2013). However, this did not mean that other less mediatised sports were not just as susceptible to match-fixing, as this chapter will hopefully illustrate by arguing the cases for tennis and snooker. The aim of this chapter is hence twofold – the first to provide insight into some of the more high-profile match-fixing cases that have been uncovered within tennis and snooker specifically and to demonstrate how each of the sport governing bodies have responded to these crises to date. The second is to reflect on a series of integrity challenges that have been raised by a number of sport stakeholders in dealing with these issues and to provide a number of recommendations on how best to go forward.

Tennis

In the UK, tennis is the third most bet on sport after football and racing among online bettors. Tournaments such as Wimbledon are highly lucrative for bookmakers with the men's final in 2007 between Roger Federer and Rafael Nadal drawing more than €44 million in wagers (Hruby, 2013). In German sports events this trend continues to manifest itself, with tennis attracting almost €1 billion annually of the total of bets placed worldwide, second only to football (Sportradar in Rebeggiani & Rebeggiani, 2013: 171). The growth of the sports betting market in

Table 3.1 Betfair's total betting volume (£) and in-play percentage for tennis (March–December 2011)

	Sport	Pre-event volume	In-play volume	Total volume	In-play %
1	Horse racing	25,328,277,899	6,403,373,114	31,737,651,012	20.2%
2	Football	6,411,511,492	8,813,420,301	15,224,921,793	57.9%
3	**Tennis**	**1,119,519,924**	**6,595,110,043**	**7,714,629,967**	**85.5%**
4	Golf	1,786,089,270	1,819,349,459	3,605,438,729	50.5%

Source: Adapted from Table compiled by Green All Over Blogspot (January 2012)

Europe has been staggering, primarily attributed to the introduction of live bets, which in tennis now amounts to almost 90 per cent of the total betting volume (IRIS, 2012: 38) as Table 3.1 illustrates.

During the past decade the integrity of tennis had been undermined repeatedly by alleged claims that tennis was being manipulated by match-fixers, but it was not until August 2007 that the public and the sport governing body took note as one of its top five world ranked players was implicated. The betting report indicated strongly that the match had been tampered with as Nikolay Davydenko, ranked fourth in the ATP ranking, withdrew from the match in the third set against a much lower-seeded opponent (Martin Vassallo Arguello – at the time ranked eighty-seventh). A total of £7 million was placed on the match with online bookmaker Betfair, with the bulk of the bets placed on a Davydenko loss. Betfair decided to void all bets on the event, despite the fact that Davydenko was eventually cleared of any wrong-doing in 2008 (*The Guardian*, 2008). Notwithstanding there was still a lurking suspicion that the game had been fixed. Following the worldwide publicity that this incident evoked, the professional tennis authorities commissioned an independent report with the aim of outlining which were the main threats to the integrity of professional tennis and providing recommendations on how best to address them. Their concerns were succinctly voiced in this report (Gunn and Rees, 2008: 21):

> The publicity given to allegedly corrupt tennis matches in recent months has been a double-edged sword. It is damaging for the reputation of the sport and can dent the confidence of sponsors, other commercial and betting stakeholders and spectators alike.

Out of the five major threats identified by the investigators betting-related corruption was highlighted in two instances. Consequently, 75 tennis matches that were played between 2003 and 2008, that reportedly had suspicious betting patterns were scrutinised and 45 of these merited further investigation. What is important to note at this stage was that the matches flagged in this report were only those reported by Betfair, a legal bookmaker which had signed a memorandum of understanding (MoU) with the Association of Tennis Professionals (ATP) in 2003. (By 2014, Betfair had signed 60 MoU with European and international sport governing bodies.) With this in mind the authors observed that 75 matches over the course of five years was a conservative number; however, they still warned that there was a strong possibility that a much larger number of matches remain at risk of match-fixing with the bets being placed with other legal and illegal operators. In conclusion the authors made 11 recommendations on how best to safeguard the integrity of tennis, with the strongest being the need to harmonise the various sets of Regulations and Codes of Conduct endorsed by a number of International Tennis Regulatory Bodies under one Tennis Anti-Corruption Programme. In line with these recommendations a Tennis Integrity Unit (TIU) was set up in 2008 with Jeff Rees (one of the principal investigators of the report) appointed as Director of Integrity. Mr Rees, a former Detective Chief Superintendent with the Metropolitan Police in London and later appointed as Chief Investigator of the International Cricket Council Anti-Corruption and Security Unit, served a four-year term until December 2012. During his tenure he established and oversaw the Uniform Tennis Anti-Corruption Program which had the following aims: 'to maintain the integrity of tennis, to protect against any efforts to impact improperly the results of any match and to establish a uniform rule and consistent scheme of enforcement and sanctions applicable to all professional tennis events and to all governing bodies' (Article X). In terms of the specific regulations governing betting-related match-fixing it foresees generally that (ATP Rulebook 2014):

> 'No Covered Person shall, directly or indirectly, wager or attempt to wager on the outcome or any other aspect of any Event or any other tennis competition.'
>
> 'display of live tennis betting odds on a Covered Person website; writing Articles for a tennis betting publication or website; conducting personal appearances for a tennis' is not allowed.
>
> '[n]o Covered Persons shall, directly or indirectly, solicit or accept any money, benefit or Consideration, for the provision of any Inside Information.'
>
> '[n]o Covered Person may be employed or otherwise engaged by a company which accepts wagers on Event.'

In the event that individuals are found in breach of these rules, they can be sanctioned for a period of up to three years and incur a fine of up to $250,000. However, in specific cases a life ban is imposed on the individual by the sport governing body. By 2012, five players and a manager had been subsequently disciplined with two of the players being banned from tennis for life (TIU Media Release, December 2012). The two players who were penalised with the harshest ban in 2011 were Austrian Daniel Koellerer (highest ranking ATP 55) and Serbian David Savic (highest ranking ATP 193) who were both charged with three offences in relation to match-fixing (TIU Media Release, October 2011). In January 2013, Mr Nigel Willerton, a former senior officer with the Metropolitan Police, succeeded Mr Rees as Director of TIU (TIU Media Release, December 2012). A third and fourth life ban was handed to two Russian players: Sergeo Krotiouk (ranked 789th in the world) who was found guilty of 41 charges relating to match-fixing, and Andrey Kumantsov, who was found guilty of 12 charges under Article D.1 of the Anti-corruption Program (Bloomberg, June 2013; TIU Media Release, June 2014). For the first time since its establishment, the TIU banned for life a French umpire, Morgan Lamri, who was found guilty of 16 separate breaches of wagering on matches (*The Washington Post*, November 2014).

In early 2014, tennis had to contend with yet another betting-related infringement as a British man was charged in Victoria (during the Australian Open tournament) with 'courtsiding', which is the act when someone present at the match can feed information into an electronic device so that someone elsewhere can use that information to bet on the outcome of a spot in an event, such as a serve. Courtsiding was made illegal in Victoria in 2013, with new laws introduced covering offences that target sports corruption and match-fixing (ABC news, 2014). Although the man was later released as he was not found to be involved in illegal gambling, this incident will surely serve as an eye-opener to tennis authorities that are constantly trying to remain abreast of the rapid technological advancement that gamblers are developing to profit from their investment. As Eaton, the integrity director at ICSS attested, courtsiding is straightforward 'cheating' as it relies on insider trading. It is basically the act of feeding live information, a fraction of the time quicker to gamblers to be able to place their bets and make a fast win (Chambers, 2014). Given this development, it remains to be seen to what extent other national jurisdictions/international governing bodies organising sporting events will draft regulations to penalise courtsiding.

Exactly two years later, on the eve of the Australian Open, the tennis world woke up to even more shocking revelations as a number of investigative journalists working for BBC and news site BuzzFeed released the most incriminating report yet. The secret files that the journalists had uncovered included evidence incriminating 16 tennis players, who were ranked in the world's top 50 of suspected match-fixing in professional tennis. To complicate matters further, the TUI failed to act on this information and left high-profile players and Grand Slam winners to continue to compete. The alleged betting syndicates that were fixing the games were traced back to Russia and Italy and had even tampered with matches at Wimbledon, one of the most lucrative events for the tennis authorities (BuzzFeed News, 2016).

World snooker

Since its inauguration as a professional sport, almost a century ago, world snooker has grown significantly both in terms of competition and public appeal. According to statistics published by its governing body, the World Professional Billiards and Snooker Association (WPSBA), it is played in over 90 countries by over 120 million players. Its flagship event the World Championship has been organised annually since 1927 and in 1985 more than 18 million spectators watched the final frame on television. The eighties marked a critical point for snooker as whole tournaments started to get televised as a result of popular appeal. Currently WPBSA estimates that they have over 450 million viewers in 78 countries worldwide (World Snooker.com, 2010a). Consequently, the winnings from this event have augmented remarkably from £6 in 1927 to £250,000 in 2013. The total prize money for professional tournaments more than doubled in 2013, increasing from £3 million to more than £7 million (World Snooker.com, 2010b).

The link between snooker and betting companies has always existed but it consolidated itself into a sponsorship deal when Betfred.com decided to sign a five-year deal to sponsor the World Championship between 2009 and 2014. In terms of betting volume, snooker features around eleventh place as Table 3.2 depicts, contributing over £120 million to Betfair's total betting volume over a nine-month period. Similar to tennis, live betting features highly in snooker, generating 83 per cent of the total betting volume.

Snooker also had to fight constant allegations of match-fixing and despite the overwhelming evidence of hard betting dating data indicative of fixing, it remained problematic to prove in court. Regardless of the complexity in collating evidence and proving such cases, the WPBSA adopted a zero tolerance approach to match-fixing and through its integrity unit attempted to remove such individuals from their sport. An

Table 3.2 Betfair's total betting volume (£) and in-play percentage by sport including tennis and snooker (March–December 2011)

	Sport	Pre-event volume	In-play volume	Total volume	In-play %
1	Horse racing	25,328,277,899	6,403,373,114	31,737,651,012	20.2%
2	Football	6,411,511,492	8,813,420,301	15,224,921,793	57.9%
3	Tennis	1,119,519,924	6,595,110,043	7,714,629,967	85.5%
4	Golf	1,786,089,270	1,819,349,459	3,605,438,729	50.5%
5	Cricket	306,559,528	3,092,151,856	3,398,711,384	91%
6	Basketball	91,342,849	292,664,626	384,007,474	76.2%
7	Rugby Union	104,999,008	78,389,521	183,388,529	42.7%
8	Darts	48,929,439	122,235,638	171,165,077	71.4%
9	American Football	63,531,264	94,110,307	157,641,571	59.7%
10	Motor Sport	73,669,130	55,494,872	129,164,002	43%
11	**Snooker**	**21,854,939**	**106,234,528**	**120,089,467**	**82.9%**

Source: Adapted from Table compiled by Green All Over Blogspot (January 2012)

anonymous hotline was set up for players and players' representatives to report any integrity issues that they come across. Since 1995, fifteen players have been investigated for match-fixing with six players found guilty of bringing the game into disrepute and breaching the WPBSA Members Rules and Regulations.

Key betting rules that are currently in operation forbid players to place, accept or lay bets in relation to the result or progress of the match and/or tournament. Directly or indirectly soliciting a bet is also penalised whether it is in return for payment or other type of remuneration or benefit. Contriving an event by offering or receiving a bribe is sanctioned under WBPSA rules, while the misuse of privileged (inside) information is also deemed as a betting misconduct (World Snooker Members Rules and Regulations, October 2014).

The harshest sanction to date went to Stephen Lee (formerly ranked fifth in the world) who was banned from snooker for 12 years and fined £40,000. Mr Lee, who had been competing on the professional snooker circuit for the past 20 years, was charged with seven counts of match-fixing dating from 2008, which led three groups of gamblers to make a total profit of £100,000 (BBC Sport, 25 September 2013a). Mr Lee later appealed this decision but was unsuccessful and was ordered to pay an additional £20,000 in costs, which took the total sum owed to the WPBSA to £125,000 (BBC Sport, 3 June 2014). According to the WPBSA the 'heavy' sanction was to convey a strong message across the snooker world and to deter anybody who would be willing to participate in such fraudulent behaviour.

The proactive efforts of the WPBSA to eradicate corruption from its sport has not stopped there as it has continued to seek ways of leading the way for other sport organisations in this area. To this end the WPBSA signed a Global Integrity Partnership with the International Centre for Sport Security (ICSS) in October 2013. Areas of collaboration are envisaged to include integrity training and education, investigation advice and support, intelligence gathering and enhancing monitoring and detection mechanisms of international snooker (World Snooker News, 2013). During the inauguration of this partnership the Chairman of the WPBSA reiterated the strong stance that the sport governing body is adopting and how such collaboration safeguards the WPBSA's position as one of the world's leading sports in anti-corruption strategies:

> We are proud to carry the global weight of the ICSS network within our sport. This new agreement with the ICSS demonstrates the WPBSA's commitment to integrity and our message to those who think about fixing matches is clear. We are watching, we will identify it, we will investigate, it has no place in our sport.

Integrity challenges: Emergent patterns identifiable across the two sports

While the current action in preventing and dealing with cases of match-fixing, being taken by the two international sporting governing bodies is debatable, there still remains a number of concerns that need to be addressed. A recent report published by ICSS (2014a) has indicated strongly that corrupt activity within sport is increasingly on the rise, claiming that organised crime launders around €100 billion annually by laying bets on sporting events. Consequently, sport governing bodies are becoming exceedingly aware not only of the risks associated with a match-fixing event but also to what extent they are being held responsible by the media and academia in allowing them to take place. To date the tendency by some sport organisations, including tennis, was to hide evidence of match-fixing. Harris (2013), an investigative journalist, has been highly critical of the way the tennis authorities continue to protect any of the detail in gathering intelligence and publishing the hearing process. Only the outcomes are made public. Although he acknowledges that the TIU commits significant time and resources in travelling to the events and interviewing suspects there is never a confirmation on how many cases they investigate per year. He contrasts this approach with other sports governing bodies such as horse-racing, cricket and snooker, which have adopted a more open approach and do publish extensive detail of individual cases of betting related corruption (*The Daily Mail*, 2013). Rodenburg and Feutsel (2014) corroborate this observation and go as far as concluding that 1 per cent of all tennis matches are fixed. They also stress that since the TIU has failed to convict any top players and/or publish any detail on the cases they investigate, they are simply not using all their power to take a strong stance against corruption. The TIU on their part continue to deny this fact and in a response to the damaging BBC and Buzzfeed claims reiterated (BBC Sport, 2016):

> The TIU and the tennis authorities absolutely reject any suggestion that evidence of match-fixing has been suppressed for any reason. The sport has a zero-tolerance approach which is enforced with the full powers of the Tennis Anti-Corruption Program, which includes lifetime bans and punitive financial penalties.

Reporting and prosecuting match-fixing cases

The media has an instrumental role to play in bringing the issues relating to match-fixing to the general public. As has been demonstrated in the case of tennis, the external pressure that the media managed to exert on the sport governing body led to the eventual establishment of the TIU. As Carpenter (2014) observed, the media tend to be one of the first to pick up on a suspicious sporting event as they are constantly present on the field of play, which they then report to the designated integrity units and/or betting regulators. During the period 1 September 2007 and 31 March 2012, 279 cases of suspicious betting were reported to the Gambling Commission governing the gambling industry in Great Britain, 191 of the cases flagged by betting operators while 88 were reported by the media, the sport governing bodies, the public or non-regulated bodies. Out of the 279 reported, 157 cases were deemed unsubstantiated (an explanation for what was considered suspicious has been found that eliminated further suspicion), 12 of which related to snooker and 20 to tennis, as Table 3.3 demonstrates.

After all intelligence received has been logged and assessed the Commission then decides on which entity is best to contact to proceed with the case. During this period 51 of these were 'passed on to the relevant sport governing body as the nature of the event is more appropriately dealt with under sport rules' (Gambling Commission 2012: 21).

The international governing bodies of tennis and snooker have adopted a different approach when it comes to sanctioning this type of

Table 3.3 Unsubstantiated suspicious betting activity (1 September 2007 to 31 March 2012)

Activity	Total cases closed to 31 Mar 2010	Cases closed 1 Apr 2010 to 30 Sep 2010	Cases closed 1 Oct 2010 to 31 Mar 2011	Cases closed 1 Apr 2011 to 30 Sep 2011	Cases closed 1 Oct 2011 to 31 March 2012	Total cases closed to 31 Mar 2012
Boxing	1	0	2	0	0	3
Cricket	1	0	2	2	0	5
Darts	2	0	0	0	0	2
Football	17	8	11	4	6	46
Golf	1	0	0	0	0	1
Rugby League	2	1	0	1	1	5
Snooker	**8**	**1**	**2**	**0**	**1**	**12**
Squash	0	0	1	0	0	1
Table tennis	0	0	0	0	0	1
Tennis	**14**	**1**	**1**	**1**	**3**	**20**

Source: Adapted from Table 23: Unsubstantiated suspicious betting activity (Gambling Commission 2012: 21)

behaviour. In tennis life bans have been handed down to players who were charged on three counts of match-fixing, while in snooker Stephen Lee was banned for 12 years notwithstanding that he was found guilty of seven charges. Following Stephen Lee's verdict, the World Snooker chairman observed that 'the courts today don't seem to like to give out lifetime bans in any sport, this seems to be the policy generally' (BBC Sport, 25 September 2013b). The disparity between the final decisions taken by the two sport governing bodies in punishing culpable individuals is worthy of note, especially when one takes into consideration that in tennis, at best the career of a professional player lasts between 10 and 15 years, while in snooker players usually compete for several decades. As Andy Murray stressed when commenting on this subject, some tennis players are more tempted to fix as they need to make all their money while they are still active (Hruby, 2013).

Episodic games and online betting

Episodic games refer to those types of sports such as cricket, tennis and snooker where an individual has almost complete control over certain plays that do not necessarily affect the outcome of the game, but are particularly susceptible to spot fixing (Asser Institute, 2014). Spot fixing can include hitting an ace in a specific game in tennis or losing a frame in snooker. Some players justify accepting to spot fix as they think there is nothing wrong in manipulating a number of isolated, seemingly innocuous, plays which have no bearing on the final result. However, such actions still give fixers an edge in the betting market given that live bets make up more than 80 per cent of the total betting volume in tennis and snooker, as explained above.

The issue is further compounded when one takes into account the nature of tennis and snooker which are both individual sports and played on professional circuits. A number of former and current athletes have acknowledged that it is easier to manipulate individual sport as opposed to team sport and the opportunities are endless given that the number of tournaments organised continues to expand. McEnroe (tennis) and Thorne (snooker), two former star players in their respective sports, conceded that matches can be easily manipulated and it is very difficult if not impossible to get caught (Hruby, 2013 and *The Telegraph*, 2011).

Vulnerable players and officials

Given the professional status of tennis and snooker and the significant media attention that their elite events enjoy, it is sometimes difficult for the public to conceive that players competing just below the ATP tour, for example, are struggling financially. This is as a result of the relatively low prize money that the Challenger Tour offers to winners, despite the fact that they still have to travel extensively to compete in tournaments and pay for their accommodation. As Chambers (2014) noted, the winner of the Challengers Tour obtained £12,000 in 2014, while the winner at Wimbledon received £1.76 million in prize money during the same year. This makes it increasingly difficult for the thousands of players, who are trying to break into the full circuit but do not have the means to finance themselves over the period that it will take to make this transition. This puts them in a highly vulnerable position, often playing into the hands of fixers, who exploit them but provide them with the much-needed cash to make it to the next tour. The study conducted by Kingston University consolidates this risk as they estimated that players ranked in the top 50 earned on average more than £700,000 annually on both the men and women's tour. Those from 51–100 earned slightly more than £140,000, while 101–250, an average of £60,000. For players ranked from 251–500, the earnings stood at £11,200 yearly. The average cost of playing tennis to cover food, travel and accommodation was calculated to be £27,100 for men and £28,100 for women in 2013 (BBC Sport, 2016).

A further layer of complexity is depicted by Rothenberg (2015) as he also compares the relatively low prize money won in the lower tiers in tennis with the money at stake for bettors. He gives the example of a match from the Challenger tournament (in Cherbourg, France) where the winner won $1,414 while more than $150,000 was wagered on a single match. This again puts pressure on the players who are coming through the amateur ranks, with some who contemplate forming partnerships with fixers thinking that they can break off this relationship once they acquire professional status. Eaton, however, warns against such behaviour as he reiterated 'Once you're compromised you're compromised for life', and therefore players should simply refrain from entering into such agreements as they will suffer severe consequences later on in their careers (Chambers, 2014).

Players are surely not the only individuals who are at risk of being approached by fixers as the referee/umpires are also prime targets, since they have control over the course and sometimes the outcome of a game. As in most other sports, snooker referees and tennis officials are particularly vulnerable given the relatively low (and sometimes late) salaries that they receive for their officiating services compared to the salaries/prize money that athletes receive (Asser Institute, 2014; Chambers, 2014). This is further exacerbated if a particular referee already has gambling-related problems and addictions, for example, which leave him/her even more vulnerable to match-fixing approaches. The Lamri case could have shed some insight into the main motivations for a tennis umpire to bet on matches but unfortunately given that the details of the hearing will remain closed, not many observations can be drawn. One could imagine, however, that given the physical proximity umpires/referees share with players and their direct knowledge of pitch conditions, injury status of players etc. could give them an edge in the betting market.

Inside information

In a report commissioned by the European Commission on preventive measures on betting-related match-fixing, it has been stated that all betting scandals, whether historic or contemporary, share a common factor and that is they have all been enabled by 'the supply of inside information' (Asser Institute, 2014: p. 10). Although, many definitions for inside information exist across all sports, it refers essentially to any type of information that is not publicly available, such as team selection news or an injury, which could influence the betting market on that particular event. The Football Association of England has taken the strongest stance to date in this matter, prohibiting everyone involved in football, including players and club managers, match officials and club staff, from passing on this type of information either 'by word of mouth, email, writing, or even social media postings' and of course from betting on the event themselves. The Rules clarify that an individual might still be in breach of the regulations, even if they did not know that the person they have passed the information to was going to use it for betting purposes (The FA Website, 2015).

In tennis, although the passing on of inside information is banned and punished, Rothenberg (2015) still insists that in many cases it goes on, seemingly unnoticed, by the relevant authorities in the lower-level pro-tournaments. Again this phenomenon is linked to the low prize money at stake in such tournaments when compared to the larger volumes that the betting market can generate and therefore the allegations are inevitable. As he reiterates: 'With alarming regularity, tennis observers have been able to tell who is going to win by spotting live betting odds that defy logic' (Rothenberg, 2015). Although, in the present conditions it is difficult to assess how widespread such links between pro players and the betting market are, consolidated action must be taken now by the respective governing body to uncover the depth of the problem and take effective measures to eradicate it.

The latest disciplinary case in snooker has also been linked to the misuse of inside information and corruption. The case was opened following suspicious betting patterns on the match between John Sutton and Jamie Burnett at the International Championship in Barnsley on 24 September 2014. Sutton, the amateur player under investigation, has been suspended from competition starting from 9 February 2015, until the conclusion of the hearing (World Snooker News, 2015). The outcome of this matter upheld that Sutton was found guilty of match-fixing and passing on inside information and is subsequently serving a six-year ban (BBC Sport, 2015). Given that the disciplinary proceeding from this case will be published in full, it would provide concrete understanding of the stance that snooker is adopting in relation to their amateur players competing for the first time on the international stage, who are found in breach of their betting rules.

Future action: Strengthening integrity

From the foregoing, it is clear that beyond suspending players from competition, there is a need to educate and train players and their entourage more effectively on issues associated with betting-related match-fixing. Such training revolves around recognising, resisting and reporting attempts to fix matches at all levels of the game. Sport governing bodies need to send a strong message in this regard and make sure that young players especially understand the difficulties that one can face. As has been highlighted by Asser Institute, sport governing bodies should not simply rely on online tools to get the message across but must engage with players face to face, by holding seminars on integrity issues during tournaments for example. To this effect, tennis has been criticised that they 'do too little' by way of education and prevention and must invest more time and resources in this area (Asser Institute, 2014: p. 114). Of course, tennis is not the only sport that is experiencing this predicament but as highlighted above, as the second most bet on sport in Europe, it definitely needs to assume a greater responsibility in educating its players and other stakeholders of the risks involved.

It is evident from the above that the integrity challenges currently plaguing tennis and snooker are complex and deeply entrenched across all levels of the sport, from amateur to elite. Hence there is no quick solution that will instantly eradicate betting-related match-fixing from their game. It is only through a structured and multi-directional management approach that tennis and snooker can tackle the sophisticated facets and dynamics of the actual integrity threats currently facing them. As profusely repeated across all reports investigating this research area (ICSS, 2014; SportRadar, 2014; Asser Institute, 2014) sport governing bodies cannot overcome these integrity challenges by themselves and therefore should seek to establish partnerships with national governments, gambling commissions and regulators, and also at supranational level, by engaging in discussions with law enforcement agencies and European institutions such as the European Commission and the Council of Europe. Through these partnerships, IFs should endeavour to become more open and facilitate discussions on the 'real' extent and depth of the integrity threats they are dealing with. This would require a complete shift in the way such cases are managed, given that a number of sport authorities tend to hide evidence of match-fixing within their sport for a myriad of reasons: some think that this is the best way to protect it, others have their own members implicated in such cases which compromise their decision to act and others unfailingly refuse to acknowledge that match-fixing is even an issue in their sport (Sportradar, 2014). Looking ahead, Sportradar has urged sport authorities to fully expose match-fixing linked to gambling and take concrete disciplinary action (e.g. banning for life from any type of involvement in that particular sport) to deter future misconduct.

As Van Rompuy (2015) avows, sport authorities should take responsibility first as they already have powerful tools (such as anti-corruption rules recently adopted by the ITF) for evidence gathering in cases of match-fixing and to sanction heavily persons found in breach of these rules. This would require another change in the approach that some of these sporting organisation have taken to date, where the tendency was to simply pass on such cases to law enforcement and prosecuting agencies arguing that they were the only ones with real investigative powers. Although criminal prosecution should follow these disciplinary proceedings, Van Rompuy (2015) insists that this not a quick fix and considering how difficult such cases are to prove in court, should provide an added incentive for sport authorities to become more proactive in dealing with such matters.

Once sport governing bodies do start taking more regulatory action in these matters they must not be complacent and need to continue to find ways to demonstrate to the public that they are becoming more open and transparent. As Hruby (2013) advocated 'transparency fosters public trust' and therefore the ITF should follow the good practice adopted by the WPBSA and publish all the details in the way they prosecute cases of match-fixing. On their part the WPBSA will need to reconsider their standpoint on life bans in snooker and ensure that the sanction imposed is proportionate to the crime committed, aligning with the strict zero-tolerance stance adopted by some of the international sport governing bodies such as football, cricket and rugby.

The issue of trust remains key. If left unchecked such betting-related cheating would seriously undermine the credibility of sport contests, which can have serious economic, legal and social repercussions for both the organisers and the public at large. If spectators suspect that particular sporting events have been fixed then their interest would decline, which can have a knock-on effect on the economic investment by the public and private market backing the event. This private investment could be in the form of sponsoring, merchandising, the betting sector and broadcasting, which can become increasingly difficult to attract if there are significantly less people interested in participating and watching sport. This phenomenon has already started to manifest itself in certain countries following a recent spate of match-fixing cases in particular sports. Rebeggiani & Rebeggiani (2013: 161) make the case for football in Italy, which is currently suffering from a sharp drop in spectator interest, with average stadium attendance falling rapidly year on year. The authors draw an interesting parallel with the case of cycling in Germany, which following the incessant doping scandals plaguing the sport in the last decade led to this decision:

In Germany, public opinion even forced public TV to stop broadcasting the *Tour de France* because the coverage of such a scandal rigged event was regarded as incompatible with a publicly funded institution.

Such a collective decision by one of the most influential sporting nations (Germany), on a high-profile individual sport such as cycling, should serve as a warning sign. Governments ultimately do have the final say, as sporting authorities cannot organise events alone, unless they have the political and financial backing of the nation. Given the substantial amount of public funding that goes into bidding, organising and delivering national and international sporting events governments need to be reassured that these sporting contests are free of cheaters as this could have a detrimental impact on their reputation. This again puts the onus on the sport governing bodies, which set the rules for their sport and are responsible for organising major sporting events worldwide. As the EU Expert Group on Good Governance in Sport attests, 'this double role of international bodies implies that standards of good governance applicable to them should be higher than those at lower levels of the sporting pyramid' (EU Expert Group, 2013: p. 4). Therefore, they must continue to strive to set the standard for good practice by demonstrating their commitment to keeping their sport clean and implementing good governance principles to mitigate the risk of betting-related match-fixing cases from reoccurring.

From the concrete actions that have been taken over the past decade by these two sport governing bodies, it is evident that there are still a number of practical measures that the tennis authorities could further take to minimise this risk. For example, re-balancing the prize money that gets distributed at the end of each tournament should go some way in helping younger and/or amateur players in being more financially independent. Although considerable effort had already been invested in this matter to bring the salaries for women equal to the men's in Tennis Majors, there still lies an alarming discrepancy in the prize money that is distributed across tournaments (*The Guardian*, 2015). Moreover, as discussed in the preceding section, the event organisers should also refrain from giving their tacit approval to the exchange of privileged information. As Rothenberg (2015) insists, the tennis authorities need to step up and intervene every time (even in lower-tier championships) there is overwhelming evidence of a fixed match. The TIU is responsible for gathering such intelligence and even though they invest a substantial budget to collect evidence, as the BuzzFeed report (2016) reveals, they have simply refused to act, year on year. Based on the way they have handled cases on betting-related match-fixing, the general feeling is that they are not independent enough to deal with such cases effectively. As alluded to earlier in the chapter, given that the international governing body and professional event organisers are the main funders of the TIU, it is not surprising that there is a clear conflict of interest in revealing too much about these cases. Therefore, a new autonomous entity along the lines of the World Anti-Doping Agency (WADA) should be considered for the dealing of betting-related match-fixing cases in the future. This would give a clear indication to the public and other stakeholders that they are treating betting-related infringements as seriously as doping. Of course, the issue of which entity will in the end fund such an initiative would still need to be debated. What is pertinent at this stage is that the international tennis federation, under the new Presidency, should take credible action to protect its clean players and convince the tennis community that it is taking every possible measure to protect its integrity!

References

ABC News. (17 January 2014). Alex McDonald, 'Man accused of courtsiding not involved in illegal gambling, employer says'. Retrieved 15 May 2015 from: www.abc.net.au/news/2014-01-17/company-who-employed-man-accused-of-courtsiding-denies-his-invo/5206028

Asser Institute. (2014). *Study on risk assessment and management and prevention of conflict of interest in the prevention and fight against betting-related match-fixing in the EU 28. Final Report.* Brussels: European Commission: DG Education and Culture. Retrieved 15 November 2015 from: http://ec.europa.eu/sport/news/2014/docs/study-asser_en.pdf

BBC Sport. (25 September 2013a). Stephen Lee: Snooker player given 12-year ban for match-fixing. Retrieved 13 April 2014, from: www.bbc.com/sport/0/snooker/24223268

BBC Sport. (25 September 2013b). Stephen Lee: reaction to 12-year snooker ban for match-fixing. Retrieved 13 April 2014, from: www.bbc.com/sport/0/snooker/24262973

BBC Sport. (3 June 2014). Stephen Lee: Banned snooker player faces £125,000 costs bill. Retrieved 4 June 2014 from: www.bbc.com/sport/0/snooker/27691612?print=true

BBC Sport. (27 May 2015). John Sutton: Snooker player given six-year match-fixing ban. Retrieved 27 May 2015 from: www.bbc.com/sport/0/snooker/32898642

BBC Sport. (19 January 2016). Tennis match-fixing 'a secret on the tour that everybody knows'. Retrieved 25 January 2016 from: www.bbc.com/sport/tennis/35356550

Bloomberg. (June 2013). Russian Tennis Player Krotiouk gets life ban for match-fixing. Retrieved 7 June 2013 from: www.bloomberg.com/news/2013-06-06/russian-tennis-player-krotiouk-gets-life-ban-for-match-fixing.html

Brasseur, A. (2012). The need to combat match-fixing, Draft resolution adopted by the Committee on Culture, Science, Education and Media, Parliamentary Assembly, Council of Europe.

Boyle, R. (2010). Sport and the Media in the UK: the long revolution? *Sport in Society: Cultures, Commerce, Media and Politics*, 13:9, 1300–1313.

BuzzFeed News. (17 January 2016). The Tennis Racket. Retrieved 20 January 2016 from: www.buzzfeed.com/heidiblake/the-tennis-racket?utm_term=.obnpoKyLa#.awxv3Oz5J

Carpenter, K. (2014). Monitoring betting at Olympic events: lessons from London 2012. *ICSS Journal*, 1(4), 84–87.

Chambers, S. (25 November 2014). Organised crime has already infiltrated tennis, says security expert. *The Guardian*. Retrieved 26 November 2014 from: www.theguardian.com/sport/2014/nov/25/organised-crime-tennis-security-expert

Chappelet, J-L. & Theodoraki, E. (2006). Key questions for policy decisions in sport in *Beyond the Scoreboard: Youth employment opportunities and skills development in the sports sector* (G. Di Cola, Editor), Geneva: ILO.

Council of Europe Parliament Assembly. (2012). Good governance and ethics in sport. Retrieved 10 October 2013 from www.assembly.coe.int/Communication/070312_RochebloineReportE.pdf

EU Expert Group (2013). Recommendations on the supervision of sports agents and on the transfers of players.

European Commission. (2014). *Study on the role of regulators for online gambling: authorisation, supervision and enforcement*. Final Study Report. Retrieved 10 March 2015 from: http://ec.europa.eu/internal_market/gambling/docs/150220-full-study-online-gambling_en.pdf.

Gambling Commission. (June 2012). Industry Statistics April 2008 to September 2011. Retrieved 5 June 2014 from www.gamblingcommission.gov.uk/pdf/Industry%20Statistics%20-%20June%202012.pdf

Green All Over Blogspot. (2012). Volume. Retrieved 22 October 2014 from: http://green-all-over.blogspot.ch/2012/01/volume.html

Gunn, B. & Rees, J. (2008). *Environmental review of integrity in professional tennis*, from: www.itftennis.com]shared/medialibrary/pdf/original/IO_32705_original.PDF.

Haberfeld, M.R. & Sheehan, D. (2013). *Match-Fixing in International Sports: Existing Processes, Law Enforcement and Prevention Strategies*. London: Springer.

Harris, N. (June 2013). Fixing, doping, whistle-blowing: secrets that tennis prefers not to discuss. Retrieved 12 March 2014 from: www.sportingintelligence.com/2013/06/24/fixing-doping-whistle-blowing-secrets-that-tennis-prefers-not-to-discuss-240601/

Hruby, P. (25 June 2013). Does tennis have a gambling problem? Retrieved 12 March 2014 from: www.sportsonearth.com/article/51670382/as-wimbledon-begins-does-tennis-have-a-gambling-problem#!UmvOB

International Centre for Sport Security – ICSS. (April 2014a). *Protecting the Integrity of Sport Competition: The last bet for modern sport.* Retrieved 2 June 2014 from: www.theicss.org/wp-content/themes/icss-corp/pdf/SIF14/Sorbonne-ICSS%20Report%20Executive%20Summary_WEB.pdf

International Centre for Sport Security – ICSS. (April 2014b). Guiding principles for protecting the integrity of sports competitions. Retrieved 2 June 2014 from: www.theicss.org/wp-content/themes/icss-corp/pdf/SIF14/Sorbonne-ICSS%20Report%20Guiding%20Principles_WEB.pdf.

INTERPOL. (2013). Match-fixing in football: Training Needs assessment. Retrieved 13 March 2014 from: www.google.ch/url?sa=t&rct=j&q=&esrc=s&source=web&cd=1&ved=0CB8QFjAA&url=http%3A%2F%2Fwww.interpol.int%2Fcontent%2Fdownload%2F22042%2F207247%2Fversion%2F4%2Ffile%2FE%2520TNA%25202013_FINAL.pdf&ei=6xYQVeLPBYL5UNT7g5gL&usg=AFQjCNEER1fMEQd-wXcQxOtWwlcCoAL7kw&bvm=bv.88528373,d.d24

Institut de Relations Internationales et Strategique – IRIS. (2012). *Sports betting and corruption: How to preserve the integrity of sport.* Retrieved 15 April 2012 from: www.2012_-_IRIS_-_Etude_Paris_sportives_et_corruption_-_ENG-1.pdf

International Olympic Committee (IOC) Press Release. (7 May 2014). IOC awards Olympic Games broadcast rights to NBCUniversal through to 2032. Retrieved 3 June 2014 from: www.olympic.org/news/ioc-awards-olympic-games-broadcast-rights-to-nbcuniversal-through-to-2032/230995

Maennig, W. (2005). Corruption in International Sport and Sports Management: Forms, Tendencies, extent and Countermeasures, *European Sport Management Quarterly*, 5:2, 187–225.

Mendick, R. (11 June 2011). 'Wimbledon Given Watchlist of Tennis Corruption Suspects'. Retrieved 1 June 2014 from: www.telegraph.co.uk/sport/tennis/wimbledon/8570017/Wimbledon-given-watchlist-of-tennis-corruption-suspects.html.

National Audit Office (NAO). (2012). The London Olympic and Paralympic Games: post-games review. Accessed 10 January from: www.nao.org.uk/publications/1213/london_2012_post-games_review.aspx

Oxford Research. (2014). Study on the sharing of information and reporting of suspicious sport betting activity in the EU 28. Retrieved 12 November 2014 from: http://ec.europa.eu/sport/news/2014/docs/oxford-vu-excecutive-summary_en.pdf.

Oxford Research. (2010). Examination of threats to the integrity of sports. Retrieved 12 May 2012 from: www.eusportsplatform.eu/Files/Filer/examination%20of%20threats%20to%20sports%20integrity.pdf

Play the Game. (2014). *Match-fixing risk at highest level in badminton exposed.* Retrieved 20 October 2014 from: http://playthegame.org/news/news-articles/2014/match-fixing-risk-at-highest-level-in-badminton-exposed/?utm_source=Play+the+Game+newsletter&utm_campaign=2c69dcfb75-Match_fixing_in_badminton10_17_2014&utm_medium=email&utm_term=0_2ff3a776de-2c69dcfb75-96736289

Rebeggiani, L. & Rebeggiani, F. (2013). Which factors favour betting related cheating in sport? Some insights from political economy, in Haberfeld, M.R. & Sheehan, D. (2013) *Match-Fixing in International Sports: Existing Processes, Law Enforcement and Prevention Strategies*, London: Springer.

Reuters. (16 January 2013). Match-fixing gangs target 50 national leagues: FIFA. Retrieved 15 March from: http://in.reuters.com/article/2013/01/16/soccer-fifa-matchfixing-idINDEE90F0AH20130116

Rodenberg, R. & Feutsel, E. (2014). Forensic sports analytics: Detecting and predicting match-fixing in tennis. *Journal of Prediction Markets*, 8(1), 77–95.

Rompuy, B. V. (2015). The Role of EU Competition Law in Tackling Abuse of Regulatory Power by Sports Associations. *Maastricht Journal of European and Comparative Law*, 22(2), 179–208.

Rothenberg, B. (2 March 2015). Game, set and (Fixed) match: Pro tennis has a match-fixing problem in its lower ranks. Retrieved 2 March 2015 from: www.slate.com/articles/sports/sports_nut/2015/02/denys_molchanov_match_fixing_allegations_pro_tennis_has_a_match_fixing_problem.html

Sportradar. (2014). *World Match-fixing: The problem and the solution*. Retrieved 30 April 2014 from: https://security.sportradar.com/sites/security.sportradar.com/files/Sportradar%20Security%20Services_World%20Match-Fixing-The%20Problem%20and%20the%20Solution.pdf

Tennis Integrity Unit (TIU) Press Release. (10 June 2014). Andrey Kumantsov found guilty of corruption offenses. Retrieved 20 March 2015 from: www.tennisintegrityunit.com/media/21/andrey-kumantsov-found-guilty-of-corruption-offenses/

Tennis Integrity Unit (TIU) Press Release. (10 December 2012). Tennis Integrity Unit confirms retirement of Jeff Rees and appointment of Nigel Willerton as new Director of Integrity. Retrieved 3 June 2014 from: www.tennisintegrityunit.com/media/16/tennis-integrity-unit-confirms-retirement-of-jeff-rees-and-appointment-of-nigel-willerton-as-new-director-of-integrity/

Tennis Integrity Unit (TIU) Press Release. (1 October 2011). David Savic anti-corruption disciplinary hearing. Retrieved 3 June 2014 from: www.tennisintegrityunit.com/media/12/david-savic-anti-corruption-disciplinary-hearing/

The Daily Mail. (8 June 2013). Match-fixing experts fear corrupt stars will be playing at Wimbledon. Retrieved 11 June 2013 from: www.dailymail.co.uk/sport/tennis/article-2338054/Match-fixing-experts-fear-corrupt-tennis-players-playing-Wimbledon-Championships.html

The FA. (2015). Rules and Governance: Inside Information. Retrieved 23 March 2015 from: www.thefa.com/football-rules-governance/betting/inside-information

The Guardian. (11 September 2015). Battle of the sexes: charting how women in tennis achieved equal pay. Retrieved 20 November 2015 from: www.theguardian.com/sport/2015/sep/11/how-women-in-tennis-achieved-equal-pay-us-open

The Guardian. (13 September 2008). Davydenko in the clear over match-fixing allegations. Retrieved 23 March, 2015 from: www.theguardian.com/sport/2008/sep/13/tennis

The Telegraph. (10 October 2011). Former snooker star Willie Thorne make match-fixing claims. Retrieved 4 June 2014 from: www.telegraph.co.uk/sport/8819193/Former-snooker-star-Willie-Thorne-makes-match-fixing-claims.html

The Washington Post. (25 November 2014). French Tennis umpire banned for life over match-fixing and other corruption charges. Retrieved 25 November from: www.washingtonpost.com/blogs/early-lead/wp/2014/11/25/french-tennis-umpire-banned-for-life-over-match-fixing-and-other-corruption-charges/

Transparency International. (No.02/2014). Working paper: Corruption and sport: building integrity to prevent abuses. Retrieved 1 September 2014, from: www.transparency.org/whatwedo/publication/working_paper_2_2014_corruption_and_sport_building_integrity_to_prevent_abu

World Snooker News. (9 February 2015). WPBSA Statement – John Sutton. Retrieved 23 March 2015 from: www.worldsnooker.com/page/NewsArticles/0,,13165~4475382,00.html

World Snooker Members Rules and Regulations: Section 2 – Betting Rules. (October 2014). Retrieved 15 March 2015 from: www.wpbsa.com/sites/default/files/uploads/members_rules_and_regulations_as_revised_october_2014.pdf

World Snooker News. (October 2013). ICSS and WPBSA announce partnership. Retrieved 21 May 2014 from: www.worldsnooker.com/page/NewsArticles/0,,13165~3496972,00.html

World Snooker. (2010a). Sponsorship Information. Retrieved 21 May 2014 from: www.worldsnooker.com/page/AboutSponsorshipInformation

World Snooker. (2010b). Snooker history. Retrieved 21 May 2014 from: www.worldsnooker.com/page/AboutHistoryofSnooker

4 Match fixing and money laundering

Jack Anderson

Introduction

This chapter is premised on the following: a conspiracy to fix or otherwise manipulate the outcome of a sporting event for profitable purpose. That conspiracy is in turn predicated on the conspirators' capacity to: (a) ensure that the fix takes place as pre-determined; (b) manipulate the betting markets that surround the sporting event in question; and (c) collect their winnings undetected by either the betting industry's security systems or the attention of any national regulatory body or law enforcement agency.

However, this contribution does not focus on the 'fix' – part (a) of the above equation. It does not seek to explain how or why a participant or sports official might facilitate a betting scam through either on-field behaviour that manipulates the outcome of a game or by presenting others with privileged inside information in advance of a game. Neither does this contribution seek to give any real insight into the second part of the above equation: how such conspirators manipulate a sports betting market by playing or laying the handicap or in-play or other offered betting odds. In fact, this contribution is not really about the mechanics of sports betting or match-fixing at all; rather, it is about the sometimes under-explained reason why match-fixing has reportedly become increasingly attractive as of late to international crime syndicates. That reason relates to the fact that given the traditional liquidity of gambling markets, sports betting can, and has long been, an attractively accessible conduit for criminal syndicates to launder the proceeds of crime. Accordingly, the term 'winnings', noted in part (c) of the above equation, takes on an altogether more nefarious meaning.

This chapter's attempt to review the possible links between match-fixing in sport, gambling-related 'winnings' and money laundering is presented in four parts.

First, some context will be given to what is meant by money laundering, how it is currently policed internationally and, most importantly, how the growth of online gambling presents a unique set of vulnerabilities and opportunities to launder the proceeds of crime. The globalisation of organised crime, sports betting and transnational financial services now means that money laundering opportunities have moved well beyond a flutter on the horses at your local racetrack or at the roulette table of your nearest casino. The growth of online gambling platforms means that at a click it is possible for the proceeds of crime in one jurisdiction to be placed on a betting market in another jurisdiction, with the winnings drawn down and laundered in a third jurisdiction and thus the internationalisation of gambling-related money laundering threatens the integrity of sport globally.

Second, and referring back to the infamous hearings of the US Senate Special Committee to Investigate Organised Crime in Interstate Commerce of the early 1950s, ('the Kefauver Committee'), this chapter will begin by illustrating the long-standing interest of organised crime gangs – in this instance, various Mafia families in the United States – in money laundering via sports gambling-related means.

Third, and using the seminal 2009 report 'Money Laundering through the Football Sector' by the Financial Action Task Force (FATF, an intergovernmental body established in 1989 to promote effective implementation of legal, regulatory and operational measures for combating money laundering, terrorist financing and other related threats to the integrity of the international financial system), this chapter seeks to assess the vulnerabilities of international sport to match-fixing, as motivated in part by the associated secondary criminality of tax evasion and transnational economic crime.

The fourth and concluding parts of the chapter spin from problems to possible solutions. The underlying premise here is that heretofore there has been an insularity to the way that sports organisations have both conceptualised and sought to address the match-fixing threat, e.g. if we (in sport) initiate player education programmes; establish integrity units; enforce codes of conduct and sanctions strictly; then our integrity or brand should be protected. This chapter argues that, although these initiatives are important, the source and process of match-fixing is beyond sport's current capacity, as are the possible solutions.

1. The link between money laundering, sports betting and match-fixing

Focusing first on money laundering; in 2012, a Senior Financial Sector Expert in the IMF's Legal Department stated bluntly: 'Money laundering is an essential component of any profit-making crime, because without laundering, crime really doesn't "pay"' (Ashin, 2012: pp. 38–39). Money laundering is a process which transforms the proceeds of crime (typically that made from the trafficking of drugs) into assets that appear legitimate in nature, e.g. property portfolios, luxury goods such as artworks or accounts at reputable banks. While the social cost resulting from drug trafficking is evident, the associated societal cost resulting from the laundering of drug monies is also significant. The laundering of such 'dirty' money perpetuates the power and influence of such criminal enterprises by resourcing the bribing and corruption of key political and law enforcement figures and thus it affords such enterprises further protection in carrying out their 'trade'. The activity also denies a country's Finance Department significant tax revenue; destabilises and deters legitimate enterprise and investment, and, in extreme cases, finances insurgency and even terrorist activities.

The link between the proceeds of crime and money laundering can be seen clearly in the most recent estimates on illicit financial flows globally. A 2011 United Nations Office on Drugs and Crime (UNODC) meta-analysis of existing estimates has suggested that criminal proceeds are, annually, now close to US$2.1 trillion or 3.6 per cent of global GDP. The best estimate for the amount available for laundering through the international financial system is the equivalent to 2.7 per cent of global GDP or US$1.6 trillion yearly (UNODC, 2011: p. 7). The starkest figure is, however, that the 'interception rate' for anti-money-laundering efforts at the global level remains critically low: only 0.2 per cent of the proceeds of crime laundered via the financial system are seized and frozen (UNODC, 2011: p. 7).

Gambling platforms of various kinds (from gaming machines to casino gambling to online sports betting exchanges) provide a unique conduit for laundering the proceeds of crime such that they emerge as legitimate business revenue. The characteristics that are most relevant include the following: liquidity is usually high; the cash flow is fluid and easily internationalised online; global sports betting law lacks harmony and enforcement is, in any event, uneven as aggravated by the fact that there is a bewildering array of regulated and unregulated bookmakers available to process bets; gambling winnings in some jurisdictions are tax free and/or can be easily diverted offshore; and the payout percentage, relative to investment returns available in other financial services industries, are high (Fielder, 2013).

In a 2011 report, SportAccord (a representative body for both Olympic and non-Olympic international sports federations as well as organisers of international sporting events) took especial care to highlight the risks emanating for the last named point above: the high payout rate. The report reiterated that for organised crime gangs money laundering is a 'cost' of doing business, which they have historically struggled to keep to below 30 per cent; consequently, it is unsurprising that given the high payout rate available in sports betting, internet sports betting becomes an extremely attractive means of laundering money. The payout rate is the average amount won by players as a share of the cumulative amount staked – sometimes called the 'return to player' rate. Average payout rates in the sports betting industry have risen from less than 80 per cent 15 years ago to a situation where, today, online betting companies generally pay out over 92 per cent of total amounts staked. The cost of laundering is thus reduced from 30 per cent to as low as 8 per cent and in turn 'gives criminals an interest in both the betting industry and sports organisations' (SportAccord, 2013: p. 31). Using statistics similar to the UNODC figures given above, SportAccord estimates that sports betting could now be used to launder more than €11,000 million worldwide and that the winnings of fixed matches could represent up to €6.8 billion or six times more than the total global trade in illegal small arms (SportAccord, 2013: p. 37).

An interesting illustration of the above points was brought out in the annual report of the US Congressional Executive Commission on China (2013: p. 190), which assessed aspects of the gambling industry in Macau, the former Portuguese colony and now a special administrative region of the People's Republic of China. The eight square kilometre peninsula is a powerhouse in the international gambling industry and in 2013 its 35 casinos brought in a record US$45 billion (£27.4 billion) in takings, up 19 per cent from the previous year. The US Congressional report expressed serious concerns about the lack of law enforcement and regulatory reporting mechanisms to combat the laundering of large amount of money out of mainland China and through a web of gambling promoters and intermediaries known as 'junkets'. The US Congressional report cited research estimating that a staggering US$202 billion in ill-gotten funds are channelled through Macau each year (US Congressional Executive Commission on China, 2013: 190, fn.49).

To recap, money laundering is an essential component to the further profitisation of transnational crime. In a scenario where, according to UN figures, 99.8 per cent of laundered criminal proceeds go unintercepted by law enforcement agencies, it would be unsurprising if gambling was not used as a laundering mechanism and especially as the betting returns can be relatively high in yield. It follows that the temptation for criminal syndicates to enhance the laundering process, and their yields, by fixing the sporting events on which they are betting, must be significant. In turn, it becomes easy to understand why leading international law enforcements agencies, such as Interpol, constantly remind international sporting bodies that neither the source nor the gravity of the match-fixing threat should be underestimated. If international criminal syndicates are so successful at both (a) trafficking drugs, weapons, commodities, wildlife, art and cultural property, human organs and people across borders, and (b) laundering the resulting proceeds, then the integrity of sport can also and easily be trafficked and exploited for criminal gain. Indeed, the Secretary General of Interpol has been quoted as saying:

> In recent years, match fixing has become a global problem... It permits organized crime the opportunity to spread worldwide its illegal and violent activities which include murder, extortion and assault and which cause tax revenue and other losses of billions of dollars every year. (Noble, 2013: pp. vi–vii)

It must be admitted here that match-fixing in sport, although almost always motivated for illegal betting purposes, can and does take place in the absence of money laundering. But equally illegal betting and fixing of sports events can and does, for the reasons previously outlined, lend itself to the laundering of money originating from the proceeds of crime.

The next two sections of this chapter illustrate the following: first, what has been described is not a modern phenomenon because sports betting's facilitation of money laundering and/or the rigging of sporting events has a long and colourful history; and second, that sport's vulnerability as a channel for criminals to launder the proceeds of their illegal activities is not just confined to gambling-related match-fixing but has an even wider corruptive base.

2. The Kefauver Committee

In the immediate post-WWII era, and prior to the Korean War's heralding of the Cold War, American public opinion turned/returned to internal matters of concern and particularly about the emerging threat of so-called national crime syndicates and the resulting gang warfare in the country's larger cities. While in the pre-War era such gangs made their money from bootlegging or the smuggling of goods such as alcohol, in the post-War era, gambling provided a much more lucrative and safer means of not only committing crime but also laundering its illicit proceeds (Fox, 1989). In 1949, the American Municipal Association, an advocacy group representing thousands of municipal authorities across the United States (and known today as the National League of Cities), petitioned the US government to investigate the perceived threat from organised crime and particularly that associated with the Italian immigrant community (US Senate Historical Office 2013: 1). In April 1950, when the body of an assassinated Kansas City gambling kingpin was found in a Democratic Party clubhouse, slumped beneath a large portrait of President Truman, political pressure on the US Congress intensified.

On 3 May 1950, the US Senate established a five-member Special Committee to Investigate Organized Crime in Interstate Commerce. US Senate Resolution 202 of 2 May 1950 facilitated the establishment of a five-person committee 'authorized and directed to make a full and complete study and investigation of whether organized crime utilizes the facilities of interstate commerce... in furtherance of any transaction which are in violation of the law of the United States... and, if so, the manner and extent which and the identity of the persons firms or corporations by which such utilisation is being made, what facilities are being used, and whether or not organized crime utilizes such interstate facilities.' The Committee, chaired by Senator Estes Kefauver, then began a 15-month investigation across 14 major US cities in which it interviewed hundreds of witnesses in open session (Wilson, 2011).

Kefauver was of no doubt that the key to the Committee's deliberations, and thus its principal investigative focus, would have to be on what he called 'the lifeblood of organised crime': interstate gambling (US Senate Historical Office 2013: 2). Through this 'key', Kefauver thought he would unlock a nationwide conspiracy between Mafia families, corrupt politicians and crooked police officers (Moore, 1974). The hearings began in Florida on 28 May 1950 and soon revealed a political and policing culture, and particularly in Miami, that not only tolerated extensive illegal gambling dens in nightclubs, at restaurants and on sidewalk vending stalls (US Senate Special Committee to Investigate Organised Crime in Interstate Commerce, 1950, Hearings, Part 1 and Part 1a), but also crystallised into direct links between illegal bookmaking syndicates and the then governor of the state, Fuller Warren (US Senate Special Committee to Investigate Organised Crime in Interstate Commerce, 1951, Final Report: pp. 73–76).

The New York hearings were particularly dramatic and focused on the so-called 'Prime Minster of the Underworld', Frank Costello, also known to law enforcement authorities across the United States as the key figure in the nation's biggest illegal gambling syndicate (US Senate Special Committee to Investigate Organised Crime in Interstate Commerce, 1950, Hearings, Part 18). The evasive raspy-voiced replies from Costello (which later influenced Marlon Brandon's delivery in *The Godfather*) eventually put Costello in jail for contempt (Wilson, 2011: pp. 733–734) but more importantly revealed the sophisticated, interlinked nature of organised crime families interests in gambling racketeering and secondary criminality including tax evasion and money laundering (US Senate Special Committee to Investigate Organised Crime in Interstate Commerce, 1951, Final Report: pp. 2–73).

Of other interest is that in the early stages of his career in the 1920s and coinciding with the Prohibition era, Costello was closely associated with Arnold Rothstein, the criminal financier widely reputed to have been involved in the 1919 Baseball World Series fix (Katcher, 1994: pp. 138–149) and also with William 'Big' Dwyer who in the 1920s was involved variously as an owner and/or rigger of National Hockey League clubs and matches (Bruno, 2013: pp. 74–83). Indeed subsequently the experience gained by Kefauver during these hearings was put into good effect a decade later when the Senator led a series of hearings into the then state of professional boxing in the US and the egregious fixing and rigging of championships in that sport under the guise of the Mob-run International Boxing Council (Mitchell, 2009: pp. 184–91).

Despite the massive public interest generated by the Kefauver Committee's hearings (the live New York hearings attracted a TV audience of near 30 million viewers) the Committee's legacy was somewhat disappointing; for instance its principal recommendation, the creation of a federal crime commission was, in effect, vetoed by J. Edgar Hoover at the FBI (Moore, 1974: p. 215). Nevertheless, the Kefauver Committee's recommendations did present a blueprint as to how cross-border illegal gambling rackets might be confronted. In a specific sense, Kefauver correctly identified that the illegal 'bookie' empire, as he called it, had 'two vulnerable points within reach of [US] Congress' power over interstate commerce: the essential flow of specialized gambling information to the bookmaker [over interstate] wire services, and this dependence on interstate [communication] facilities in placing lay-off and come-back bets' (US Senate Special Committee to Investigate Organised Crime in Interstate Commerce, 1951, Final Report: p. 88). The Committee drafted legislative bills to strike at these points and, although never introduced, they remain instructive because today international criminals make similar use of the opportunities offered by the global, online financial system as powered by sophisticated computerised data processing and utilising offshore tax havens and legitimate investment fund accounts.

Almost a decade later, the Kennedy Administration in the US in 1960 did to some extent pick up on the recommendation of the Kefauver

Committee by way of the Federal Wire Act of 1961 (18 U.S.C. ch. 50 §1081 et seq.). That Administration recognised that that interstate gambling by electronic means was effectively underwriting large-scale criminal activity in the US (Schwartz, 2010). The Act sought to target such activity in the following manner:

> Whoever being engaged in the business of betting or wagering knowingly uses a wire communication facility for the transmission in interstate or foreign commerce of bets or wagers or information assisting in the placing of bets or wagers on any sporting event or contest, or for the transmission of a wire communication which entitles the recipient to receive money or credit as a result of bets or wagers, or for information assisting in the placing of bets or wagers, shall be fined under this title or imprisoned not more than two years, or both.

Nevertheless, as the Kefauver Committee had also realised, criminal prohibitions such as the above were a rather blunt and ineffective means of combating interstate economic conspiracy such as that involving illegal gambling. A package of legal remedies was necessary, including civil law actions and licensing regimes. Arguably, therefore, the long-term legacy of the Kefauver Committee can be seen in the Organized Crime Control Act of 1970 (better known as Racketeer Influenced and Corrupt Organizations or RICO Act of 1970, 18 U.S.C. ch. 96 § 1961 et seq.), a celebrated US federal law that provides for extended criminal penalties and a civil cause of action for acts performed as part of an ongoing criminal organisation and aims to eradicate organised crime by attacking the sources of its revenue, such as illicit gains and laundering of monies through gambling or bookmakers. Moreover, section 224 of the Act was one of the first statutory provisions worldwide specifically to target sports bribery:

> Whoever carries into effect, attempts to carry into effect, or conspires with any other person to carry into effect any scheme in commerce to influence, in any way, by bribery any sporting contest, with knowledge that the purpose of such scheme is to influence by bribery that contest, shall be fined under this title, or imprisoned not more than 5 years, or both.... As used in this section – The term 'sporting contest' means any contest in any sport, between individual contestants or teams of contestants (without regard to the amateur or professional status of the contestants therein), the occurrence of which is publicly announced before its occurrence.

In sum, the most enduring element of the collective Kefauver hearings was twofold. First, it gave the US public 'its first glimpse into the shadow economy of the underworld' and the figures were staggering: the Kefauver committee estimated conservatively that the annual illegal gambling take in the US in the early 1950s was between US$15 and 20 billion, which was about 10 per cent more that the total federal budget on military spending at the time (Russo, 2001: p. 270). Second, the Kefauver hearings also revealed an ingrained ethos of corruption in sport nationally. In the 1960s, when, as previously mentioned, Kefauver returned to sport in a series of Congressional hearings on the state of professional boxing, he revealed a sport that was an administrative and structural mess (US Senate Committee on the Judiciary, 1960). Corruption and outright criminality was rife, as indexed against poor governance and accountability in key self-regulatory aspects of the sport as aggravated by political and even law enforcement authorities nationwide. Again, the lifeblood of this sports-related crime syndicate in boxing, manifesting itself in the widespread rigging of championship bouts, was gambling.

3. Money laundering through the football sector by the FAFT

In July 2009, the Financial Action Task Force published a major study on money laundering through the professional football industry (FAFT 2009). The study claimed that money laundering through the football sector was 'deeper and more complex than previously understood' (FAFT, 2009: p. 4) and highlighted weaknesses in football's governance structures which made it attractive to criminal syndicates and including: private equity investment in or sponsorship of football clubs; third party ownership of the players' economic rights; unregulated agents manipulating the transfer market; and tax evasion by way of the exploitation of players' image.

The FAFT Report also highlighted sports betting as an area susceptible to money laundering (FAFT, 2009, pp. 24–25). In this, the FAFT Report made four points of interest.

First, it noted a matter that is sometimes underplayed in the debate on illegal betting and match-fixing: sport has always had an 'ambiguous 'and even interdependent relationship with betting. The FAFT Report pointed out that betting has historically been an important revenue source for sport in many countries (through, for instance, state-imposed betting tax levies redirected to sport's benefit). Indeed for some sports, e.g. horse racing, betting is the sport's raison d'être. In a more modern sense, as traditional sources of sponsorship for sport (such as tobacco and drinks companies) have been prohibited from being commercially associated with sport on public health grounds, sports betting companies have filled the gap left on a club's jersey. The potential conflict of interest here is a matter that needs further debate. In the same year as the FAFT was published the Court of Justice of the European Union observed as follows Case C-42/07 *Liga Portuguesa de Futebol* [2009] ECR I-7633 at para [71]:

> Moreover the possibility cannot be ruled out that an operator which sponsors some of the sporting competitions on which it accepts bets [the stated case involved Bwin, a well-known European based on-line gaming undertaking and significant sponsor of football, basketball and motor sport clubs and competitions], and some of the teams taking part in those competitions may be in a position to influence their outcome directly or indirectly and thus increase its profits.

The second point of interest is that the FAFT Report admitted that while problems linked to betting on sport 'are not new', the increasingly transnational nature of the betting industry and the 'use of the Internet for online betting further increase the risk of money laundering' (FAFT, 2009: 24). In this, the FAFT reiterated a point made earlier in this chapter: the attractiveness of the gambling markets to criminals as a means of money laundering (and concomitantly the difficulties in combatting it) must be seen in context and namely that the global gambling market is largely a non-transparent and heterogeneous market with a mix of private and state companies acting both nationally and internationally and with varying degrees of regulation ranging from the liberal to the prohibitionist and frequently operating online and offshore or both. The hotchpot nature of the global gambling industry means that proposals for a World Anti-Corruption Agency along the lines of the World Anti-Doping Agency's remit (that of harmonising anti-doping policies in global sport) is distractingly ambitious.

The third point of interest is that the FAFT focused on the involvement of Asian criminals and the region's gambling markets as a source of illegal football betting. In this regard, the FAFT report highlighted the successful actions of Interpol in combating illegal gambling activities of criminal syndicates in Asia – collectively called 'Operation Soga'. According to Interpol's 'Integrity in Sport' website, as of 2013, the four Soga operations since 2007 have resulted in 2,360 successful raids and the closure of illegal gambling dens which handled illegal bets worth more than US$2 billion; and the seizure of more than US$27 million in cash from illegal gambling operators.

The final point of interest from the FAFT report is the view that 'illegal football gambling does not necessarily only involve Asian criminals. On the contrary, most of the Asian bookmakers are professional and well organised companies with a lot of expertise in the field' (FAFT, 2009: p. 25). Problems arise because such bookmakers rarely deal directly with large, criminally exposed punters, but only by means of a network of intermediaries. This network can stretch from criminal syndicates based in Asia to gangs based in Eastern Europe, who in turn target players and clubs for fixing purposes. This is an important point. Some commentators are dismissive of any hope of confronting the match-fixing threat to sport because they say it emanates from the unregulated Asian gambling markets and yet it must be remembered that Asian bookmakers, although not as tightly supervised as those in European jurisdictions, are not operating in a totally 'hidden market'. Many, in jurisdictions such as Singapore, operate openly and professionally. It is the criminal, shadowy web of intermediaries wherein lies the problem (Hill, 2008, 2013).

Conclusion: If sport goes it alone, it will fail

Transnational organised crime gangs operate within the abovementioned web of gambling intermediaries, and these gangs have identified sports organisations as providing excellent cover for their activities (SportAccord, 2013: p. 34 and Australian Crime Commission, 2011 and 2013): sports organisations and players generally have a good public image and therefore investment in a club presents both money and/or 'image' laundering opportunities for criminals; sports bodies sometimes suffer from intrinsic structural and governance fragilities and are either weak in international organisation (e.g., professional boxing) or, with unnecessary fierceness, protect their domestic regulatory independence and hence seek to operate outside the norms of domestic public law (e.g., football) despite receiving million in public monies to facilitate large-scale international sport events. In sum, this means that sometimes there is less transparency and fewer controls in the close-knit regulatory landscape of international sport (Transparency International, 2009).

Moreover, and at both a national and international level, sports governing bodies are only now beginning to operate in a collective, consensual manner to address this integrity threat to sport and thus at present there are markedly differing levels of integrity oversight in professional sport. In addition, transnational organised crime syndicates, experienced in the trafficking of narcotics, are aware that individual, aspiring professional athletes, many of whom lack significant formal education, may be susceptible to exploitation. Many young athletes are not well represented, if at all, by their (un)regulated agents. Meaningful, representative player unions do not exist in some sports and thus some athletes are vulnerable to being 'groomed' as 'gambling mules' for future criminally-related betting scams.

With specific regard to money laundering and match-fixing but also to the match-fixing in sport debate more generally, sport should look to external expertise and should do so in three ways.

Recommendations

Recommendation 1: corruption and poor governance reflected in opaque accountability and transparency standards in administrative bodies is not the sole preserve of sport; neither are transnational criminal offences involving large-scale, criminal syndicates. Corruption in the public sector and corruption relating to transnational economic crime has been widely analysed and in this the applicability of anti-money laundering measures in, for instance, international legal instruments such as United Nations Convention against Transnational Organized Crime and the United Nations Conventions against Corruption should be given greater consideration (UNODC & IOC, 2013).

Recommendation 2: money laundering through gambling outlets results in financial and credibility detriment to gambling companies and the industry's regulators. Consequently both have advanced means of tracking and mitigating the money laundering threat, which could be usefully adapted to sport's needs, e.g. see the anti-money laundering guidelines of the Remote Gambling Association (a London and Brussels-based trade association whose membership are all licensed for gambling purposes in Europe and includes most of the world's largest and most respected internet gambling companies) and the guidance provided by the UK Gambling Commission on anti-money laundering initiatives. Both are examples of best practice (RGA, 2010 and UK Gambling Commission, 2013).

Recommendation 3: this brief chapter argues that match-fixing in sport should be placed firmly within the international discourse on transnational financial services fraud. This would not, as some might have it, unnecessarily conflate or exaggerate the seriousness of match-fixing in sport; rather the recognition of the true global extent of match-fixing in sport would be the first necessary step in the fight back by sport against the fixers. It would allow sport access to (a) the anti-corruption research (funded by entities such as the EU Commission (2011, para 4.5)), the resources (that can be brought to bear by organisations such as the aforementioned UNODC); and (b) the expertise available at intergovernmental level (epitomised by that carried out by FAFT and Interpol) that already exists in this area. Crucially, by properly describing match-fixing in sport as being characteristic of the opportunism of transnational organised crime syndicates, this might also help explain at governmental level how the integrity threat to sport is not just something that narrowly concerns the insularity or specificity of sport but is also one that necessitates wider societal concern and deeper investigative resourcing.

Finally, on 12 May 2016, the then UK Prime Minister David Cameron hosted a landmark international anti-corruption summit in London, which sought to 'galvanise' a global response to tackle corruption across a range of areas and including corporate secrecy, government transparency, the enforcement of international anti-corruption laws, and the strengthening of international institutions (Anti-Corruption Summit: London 2016). One of the areas included was sport and in the Conference's subsequent Communiqué, paragraphs 23–24 stated the following, which encapsulated much of what this piece has attempted to address. The outworkings of this communiqué and its commitments, notably an International Sport Integrity Partnership, are awaited with interest.

> [23] There is no place for corruption in Sport. High-level corruption in sports administration, match fixing, procurement, endorsement deals, site selection, illegal betting and doping, and the involvement of organised crime, have damaged the credibility of sporting bodies. They must be decisively addressed through a coordinated response. We welcome the work of the international sports organisations to strengthen openness and improve governance so that they meet global best practice. We urge them to achieve the highest global standards and regain public trust through a culture of good governance. We recognise the autonomy of international sports organisations conferred under national laws. We believe this must be exercised responsibly and be earned by continually demonstrating good governance in a spirit of openness.

> [24] We welcome the discussions, bringing together international sports organisations, governments and relevant international organisations with other stakeholders leading up to the summit, to help tackle corruption in sport. We also welcome the intention to launch an International Sport Integrity Partnership (in the margins of a meeting of the International Forum for Sport Integrity in Lausanne in early 2017). We will work with international sports organisations and other key stakeholders to support and strengthen

efforts to implement high standards of transparency and good governance, and to underpin the wider fight to eliminate corruption from sport. We will encourage good governance within national sports organisations (including through educational and capacity building initiatives) and improve information sharing between international sports organisations and law enforcement agencies. We will take legislative or other measures to combat practices such as match-fixing, illegal betting and doping, and will put in place measures to protect 'whistleblowers' from discriminatory and retaliatory actions. We will consider extending the definition of Politically Exposed Persons to include senior members of international sporting federations. International organisations will assist by taking action, such as developing codes of best practice and accountability frameworks for individual institutions, and by supporting the development of international legal frameworks.

References

Anti-Corruption Summit: London. (12 May 2016). *Communique*. Cabinet Office, UK Prime Minister's Office: London. Retrieved from: www.gov.uk/government/publications/anti-corruption-summit-communique

Ashin, P. (June 2012) Dirty Money, Real Pain. *Finance and Development*, 49(2), 38–41.

Australian Crime Commission. (2011). *Threats to the Integrity of Professional Sport in Australia: A Factsheet*. Canberra: ACC.

Australian Crime Commission. (2013). *Organised Crime and Drugs in Sport*. Canberra: ACC.

Bruno, J. (2013). *Mobsters, Gangs, Crooks and Other Creeps: Volume 2*. Charleston, SC: CreateSpace.

EU Commission. (2011). Communication form the Commission to the European Parliament, the Council, the European Economic and Social Committee and the Committee of the Regions: Developing the European Dimension in Sport. Brussels: COM(2011) 12 final. Retrieved from http://ec.europa.eu/sport/policy/organisation_of_sport/match_fixing_en.htm

Fiedler, I. (2013). Online Gambling as a Game Changer to Money Laundering? Retrieved from http://ssrn.com/abstract=2261266 & http://dx.doi.org/10.2139/ssrn.2261266

Financial Action Task Force (2009). *Money Laundering through the Football sector*. Available on www.fatf-gafi.org/media/fatf/documents/reports/ML%20through%20the%20Football%20Sector.pdf

Fox, S. (1989). *Blood and Power*. New York: William Morrow & Company.

Hill, D. (2008) *The Fix*. Toronto: McClelland & Stewart.

Hill, D. (2013) *The Insider's Guide to Match-Fixing in Football*. Toronto: Anne-McDermid.

Kathcher, L. (1994). *The Big Bankroll: The Life and Times of Arnold Rothstein*. Boston, MA: Da Capo Press.
Mitchell, K. (2009). *Jacobs Beach: The Mob, the Garden, and the Golden Age of Boxing*. London: Yellow Jersey Press.
Moore, W. (1974). *The Kefauver Committee and the Politics of Crime, 1950–1952*. Columbia, MO: University of Missouri Press.
Noble, K. (2013). 'Preface', in Haberfeld, M.R. and Sheehan, D. (Eds). *Match-Fixing in International Sports*. New York: Springer, vii–viii.
Remote Gambling Association. (2010). *Anti-money laundering: Good Practice Guidelines for the Online Gambling Industry*. London: RGA.
Russo, G. (2001). *The Outfit*. New York, Bloomsbury.
Schwartz, D. (2010). Not Undertaking the Almost-Impossible Task: The 1961 Wire Act's Development, Initial Applications, and Ultimate Purpose. *Gaming Law Review and Economics*, *14*(7), 533–540.
SportAccord. (2011). *Integrity in Sport: Understanding and Preventing Match-fixing*. Lausanne: SportAccord.
Transparency International. (2009). *Working Paper No.03/2009: Corruption and Sport: Building Integrity and Preventing Abuses*. Berlin, TI.
UK Gambling Commission. (2013). Anti-Money Laundering: Approach to Supervision, London, Gambling Commission. Retrieved from www.gamblingcommission.gov.uk/money_laundering
United Nations Office on Drugs and Crime. (2011). Estimating Illicit Financial Flows Resulting from Drug Trafficking and other Transnational Organised Crimes: Research Report. Vienna: UNODC.
United Nations Office on Drugs and Crime & International Olympic Committee. (2013) Criminalization Approaches to Combat Match-fixing and Illegal/irregular Betting: A Global Perspective. Lausanne: IOC and Vienna: UNODC.
US Congressional Executive Commission on China. (2013). Annual Report. Washington DC: US Government Printing Office.
US Senate Committee on the Judiciary. (1960). Professional Boxing: Hearing of SR 238 before the Subcommittee on Antitrust and Monopoly of the Senate Committee on the Judiciary. 86th Cong., 2nd Sess.
US Senate Historical Office. (2013). Notable Senate Investigations: Special Committee on Organized Crime in Interstate Commerce. Washington, DC: US Senate Historical Office.
US Senate Special Committee to Investigate Organised Crime in Interstate Commerce. (1950). Hearings Before Special Committee pursuant to Senate Resolution 202. Washington DC, US Government Printing Office.
US Senate Special Committee to Investigate Organised Crime in Interstate Commerce. (1951). Final Report of Special Committee pursuant to Senate Resolution 202. Washington DC, US Government Printing Office.
Wilson, T. (2011). 'The Kefauver Committee on Organized Crime, 1950–1951', in Burns, R., Hostetter, D. and Stocks, R. (Eds.). *Congress Investigates: A Critical and Documentary History*. New York: Facts on File, 715–737.

5 Integrity challenges for protection of minors
Australian compromises on sports broadcasting betting advertising

Linda Hancock

Introduction

Internationally, internet-enabled sports betting has undergone steep growth over recent years, from a lower base than other more established forms of gambling. This chapter assesses government, regulator and gambling industry commitments to integrity, conceptualised as the moral and ethical obligations to protect consumers and the vulnerable (especially children) from harm, under the license to operate. In countries like the UK and Australia, liberalised broadcasting regulation has enabled the sports betting industry to exploit gaps in provisions designed to protect children from exposure to normalisation of gambling. Pro-gambling advertising has become controversial (ACMA, 2013; Chapman, 2015; Griffiths, 2007; Loeliger, 2013; Parliament of Australia, 2013). An Australian case study highlights flawed attempts to curb sports television betting advertising during family viewing times, as a means of illustrating how integrity processes are deficient in terms of protecting young people from exposure to gambling. The corporate political activity (CPA) framework (Savell et al., 2014) is applied to the reform process 2013–2015, involving national Parliament of Australia inquiries into Advertising and Promotion of Gambling Services in Sport, to understand the strategies and tactics used by the gambling industry to influence government and regulators. This chapter discusses changing technology and risk from online gambling, youth's vulnerability to gambling advertising and gambling-related harms, the context of gambling and sports betting in Australia and focuses on a case study of sports betting advertising reforms in Australia and the application of corporate political activity (CPA) analysis to Australian Sports broadcasting policy reforms. Corporate political activity (CPA) analysis is applied to Australian Sports broadcasting policy reforms 2015–16. CPA is used as an analytical framework to understand corporate strategies aimed at influencing regulation. CPA analysis helps explain brokered deals between the gambling industry and governments and the complexity of outcomes involving powerful coalitions of vested interests.

Changing technology and risk from online gambling

Risks to minors and other vulnerable groups are heightened in the context of new online technology, which is broadening gambling accessibility and raising new issues for regulation and consumer protection. In contrast, other forms of gambling are located in venues such as casinos, clubs, hotels, kiosks and convenience stores. In land-based venues, staff can play a role in preventing access by minors and implementing responsible gambling codes of practice (leaving aside issues of how well this is done). Internationally, wagering (which encompasses sports betting) has moved to remote forms of access via telephone, internet and internet-enabled devices such as iPads and tablets, smoothing the way to expansion of internet-based sports gambling. While the ramped-up frequency of gambling industry marketing conferences on these new gambling platforms reflects industry excitement at this growing market, these trends pose new regulatory and public protection issues. This is partly because compared to land-based gambling, online/internet gambling is a more globalised virtual industry that crosses national regulatory boundaries; thus posing new challenging issues for national regulators used to land-based licensing. It is also challenging because of evidence, for example in the UK, Canada and internationally, of the harmful effects of internet gambling, which may be reaching new, younger audiences with proof of age an associated concern, and accessibility a key factor (Gainsbury et al., 2011; Griffiths, 2003, 2007; Monaghan, Derevensky & Sklar, 2008; Thomas et al., 2016; Wood & Williams 2009).

In a 2007 international self-administered survey of 12,521 internet gamblers from 105 countries, Wood and Williams found that internet gamblers were more likely to be male (78 per cent), employed, younger age, higher household income and better educated and with higher levels of gambling expenditure than non-internet gamblers; and with poker the most popular form of online gambling (Wood & Williams, 2009: pp. 8–10). Internet gamblers preferentially used online gambling for sports betting (and 17 per cent of international online gamblers bet on sports). Pointing to the heightened risks, internet gamblers had higher levels of expenditure[1] and prevalence of problem gambling three to four times higher, than non-internet gamblers. In terms of signalling increased problems from sports betting, Canadian research found that help-seeking for sports betting-related problems significantly increased from 2006 (2.7 per cent) compared with 2012 (7.6 per cent) (Ontario Problem Gambling Research Centre, 2013: n.p.).

New online gambling markets raise integrity challenges for governments, the gambling industry and regulators. For example, in 2009 the European Parliament Resolution passed a resolution on the Integrity of Online Gambling:

> integrity in the context of this resolution on online gambling means a commitment to preventing not only fraud and crime but also problem gambling and under-age gambling by compliance with consumer protection and criminal laws and by protecting sporting competitions from any undue influence *associated* with sports betting. (European Parliament, 2009, at para I)

As the European Parliament further notes, citing UK Gambling Commission research, online gambling combines several risk factors related to problem gambling, such as easy access to gambling, the availability of a variety of games and fewer social constraints. Compared with land-based gambling in venues, new online gambling technology is more accessible to under-age users and requires new regulatory thinking on how to regulate for probity, harm prevention and surveillance of participation by minors. The Parliament notes that 'whereas Member States have regulated their traditional gambling markets in order to protect consumers against addiction, fraud, money-laundering and match-fixing… these policy objectives are more difficult to achieve in the online gambling sector' (European Parliament, 2009, at para F). Subsequently, the European Parliament reiterated concerns about match-fixing and corruption in sport in a Commission Green Paper in 2011 and a European Parliament resolution on online gambling in the internal market (European Parliament, 2013). The rapid growth of internet gambling with annual growth rates of 15 per cent, estimated revenue in 2015 of EUR 13 billion compared to EUR 9.3 billion in 2011, constituting growth of about 40 per cent between 2011 and 2015 (European Parliament, 2018). Given that 75 per cent of six to seventeen year olds in Europe use the internet, they also highlight the need to protect minors and other vulnerable groups from accessing gambling (European Parliament, 2018 update of 2012/2322(INI) – 23/10/2012) and flagged the need for a Recommendation on responsible gambling advertising to be drafted. Even if rather limp, this Recommendation has subsequently directed Member States to 'ensure that minors are not able to gamble online, and that rules are in place to minimise their contact with gambling, including through advertising or promotion of gambling services whether broadcast or displayed' (European Commission, 2014).

Youth's vulnerability to gambling advertising and gambling-related harms

Internationally, despite regulatory variations, there is widespread agreement on age limits to participation in gambling, as a potentially risky adult activity. In the US it is 21 years of age, in the UK, 18 (except for lotteries and arcade games), Australia 18, Canada 18 or 19 (depending on the province), and in Macau, people must be over 21 to enter casinos. This reflects the moral and ethical commitment of governments and regulators to protection of minors as vulnerable persons.

In the UK, this is expressed formally in the third licensing objective of the Gambling Act 2005, which specifies protecting children and other vulnerable persons from 'gambling-related harms'. Echoing the sentiment expressed across many jurisdictions, the Gambling Commission has emphasised: 'The requirement in relation to children is explicitly to protect them from being harmed or exploited by gambling' (Bolton Council, 2012: p. 2).

In Australia, the overriding principle is also one of protection from harm on public health and consumer protection grounds. As articulated by the internationally acclaimed Australian Productivity Commission report (2010: p. 3.1), '(t)here are strong rationales for government regulatory and policy involvement in gambling, including the need to ensure probity and to avoid harm to consumers'. They observe children need to be protected and that '(c)ommunity norms may reasonably provide a rationale for some restrictive regulations, such as in relation to access [to gambling] by children' and in relation to advertising inappropriately attracting children to gambling (Productivity Commission, 2010: 3.6; 8.26).

Impact research has shown the vulnerability of youth to gambling participation and problems. Minors are engaging in gambling and experiencing 'more gambling-related problems than any other age cohort', with similar trends evident in Australia, Canada, the US, the UK and Norway (Monaghan, Derevensky & Skylar, 2008: p. 253). Problem gambling among adolescents has been associated with a number of adverse health outcomes, with personal, health and social consequences (Griffiths, 2003; Messerlain, Deverensky and Gupta, 2005; Monahan, 2008) and increased likelihood of criminal behaviour

Integrity challenges for protection of minors 83

and other negative impacts (Delfabbro et al., 2009). The consequences of gambling-related problems can be serious for youth and the damage can be devastating to the adolescent, peers and family. There is also evidence that adults with gambling problems develop these behaviours during adolescence (Delfabbro et al., 2009).

Research reinforces the need for interventions to prevent early exposure to gambling. Victorian Responsible Gambling Research Foundation (2013a, n.p.) research indicates: one in five adults with gambling problems started gambling before they were 18; 3–4 per cent of teenagers have problems with gambling (one in every high school class of 25 students); teenagers are four times more likely to develop gambling problems than adults and boys are more likely to gamble and develop problems than girls. Research has also identified gambling advertising as a risk factor for youth (Delfabbro et al., 2009; Deverensky et al., 2010; Griffiths, 2007; Monahan, 2008; Productivity Commission, 2010; Thomas, 2012; Thomas et al., 2016). Research by the Victorian Responsible Gambling Foundation indicates that children are more vulnerable to advertising, and that younger children aged under 11 struggle to distinguish between advertising and program content (Phillips, 2013: p. 1). Moreover, adolescents are 'particularly attuned to gambling advertisements' (Monaghan, Derevensky & Sklar, 2008: p. 263).

Canadian researchers argue that high levels of exposure to advertising creates attitudes in those aged 13–18 that gambling is 'entertaining, harmless and convivial' (McMullan, Miller & Perrier, 2012: p. 843). Canadian research found that 42 per cent of youth between the ages of 10 and 15 years, said they were influenced by gambling advertisements on television, making them want to gamble (McMullen et al., 2012: p. 830). In addition, the same authors found that most youth felt gambling-related advertisements conveyed the message that gambling is both entertainment and an opportunity to make some quick money (McMullen et al., 2012, p. 843). Thomas et al. (2016) found that marketing of sports betting brands impacts on children's recall of betting brands within sport. Others have found that males in particular have recall of the content of gambling advertising, especially for sports betting, horse/dog racing and TAB (Griffiths, 2007). Gambling advertisements also promote a wider culture of gambling normalisation, where gambling is accepted as a normal and legitimate behaviour (Fried, Techman and Rahav, 2010, p. 594; Derevensky et al., 2010, p. 23).

In jurisdictions like the UK and Australia, sports betting advertising has been controversial, through complacent government regulation and industry exploitation of gaps in regulation (Hancock and Smith, 2017a, b). In the UK, the Labour government's 2007 liberalisation of television advertising regulation allowed gambling advertising during sporting events at any time of the day, while restricting other gambling advertising to after the 9pm watershed. In 2015, an 'explosion of aggressive advertising' with a 1500 per cent increase in gambling commercials during sporting events since 2007, reportedly 'split the Coalition', with critics objecting to representation of gambling as 'a fun, everyday activity' and delays in release of a review of gambling advertising (Chapman, 2015).

Concerns about child and under-age exposure to gambling, relate not only to direct advertising (Griffiths, 2003), but to more subtle marketing via logos on team clothing and stadium hoarding advertising, visible during televised play and new platforms such as internet interactive (smart) phones widely used by young people. This renders them reachable by marketing delivered by internet during sporting events (such as stadium smartphone apps linked to betting company direct advertising, offers of credit and other incentives to gamble) (Hing et al., 2014). These new platforms may be accessed anywhere at any time, making them difficult for parents to supervise, and open to exploitative age-insensitive marketing. They make instant betting easily accessible and are rapidly gaining market traction. About one third of people who engage in sports betting in Australia place bets over the internet (The Social Research Centre 2013, p. 88). The combination of increased exposure to advertising, loosening of regulation and new gambling platforms, has been linked to increased prevalence of sports betting-related problems. University of Sydney Gambling Clinic reported an increase in the presentation of problematic sports betting gamblers from 5 to 15 or 20 per cent of clients over a six-year period, 2006–2013 (using Australian-based legal betting sites); and also noted the negative impact of sports betting advertising on recovering gamblers (Parliamentary Joint Select Committee on Gambling Reform, 2013: p. xv; pp. 27–28).

In short, sports betting gambling is associated with identifiable harms, especially for minors. Jurisdictions have implemented various measures to identify, mitigate, reduce and prevent harms (although these are yet to be fully articulated in respect of online gambling and are not necessarily well-enforced). In wide-ranging jurisdictions, youth are identified as a particularly vulnerable group in need of age-related prohibitions on access to gambling and other protective measures, including limits on sports betting advertising during general viewing times. The impacts on youth can be damaging, prompting early onset of gambling problems and associated negative impacts, especially in relation to internet gambling and the fast-growing platform of sports betting. Gaps in regulation have been exploited via new diverse and far-reaching forms of gambling marketing and advertising.

The regulatory context of gambling and sports betting in Australia

In terms of the regulatory context, gambling regulation in Australia is a mix of State/Territory and national responsibility. Regulation and licensing of gambling (e.g. venue licensing, wagering (including horse and greyhound racing), codes of practice and regulation of liquor licensed premises), are matters for State/Territory governments. Issues coming under national regulation include broadcasting, consumer protection and online gambling. The national Interactive Gambling Act 2001 sought to ban online gambling services (for example, poker and casino games) being offered in Australia, with exemptions for wagering (including sports betting) via internet, telephone or digital television (Responsible Gambling Advocacy Centre, 2011: p. 2). In terms of internet gambling, there is thus a complicated picture where some forms, such as wagering, are permitted and others (casino and poker) are not. Similar to other jurisdictions, the borderless nature of the internet makes implementation of the Act complicated by the accessibility of international online gambling providers, and opportunities for gambling via internet-enabled technologies such as mobile phones, iPads and so on.

Governments are important enforcers of integrity but have complicated relationships with the gambling industry as corporate influencers of policy, and in terms of the potential, perceived and real conflicts of interest, created by government reliance on gambling tax revenues and corporate electoral donations to political parties. In Australia, State/Territory governments are the beneficiaries of gambling tax revenue, which was over five billion dollars for the year 2008–09 (an amount similar to that spent on alcohol). States thus have considerable vested interest in gambling taxes, which contribute approximately 10 per cent of State/Territory revenue nationally (Productivity Commission, 2010: p. 7). Online bookmakers are licensed to operate out of Northern Territory and Tasmania but, post-2008, have access to a national betting market.

Gambling in sport is thus a relatively new form of wagering compared with traditional and declining horse and dog racing. It has had a steep increase but from a low base and represents a new market for the industry. According to the Productivity Commission, online sports wagering accounts increased 103 per cent and the amount spent on online sports wagering increased 73 per cent between 2004 and 2009 (2010, p. 2.39 citing iBus Media submission 178). While overall participation in gambling has decreased from 82 to 64 per cent between 1999 and 2010 (and participation in EGM gambling declined from 40 to 20 per cent), the rate of sports betting more than doubled from 6 to 13 per cent (Gainsbury cited by Seccombe, 2014: n.p.). National Australian Gambling statistics on the percentage change in gambling turnover from 2014–15 to 2015–16, show that betting expenditure increased 35 per cent over this period (Queensland Government Statistician's Office, 2017, summary table C).

In terms of the social cost of gambling in Australia, problem gambling has been associated with negative physical, health, social and economic problems including suicide, depression, relationship breakdown, lower work productivity, job losses, bankruptcy and crime (Productivity Commission, 2010: p. 16). Australians spent $1,272.8 per year per person on gambling in 2015–16 (Queensland Government Statistician's Office, 2017, summary table E), which is higher than in many other countries.[2] It also affects others such as family members, friends, employers and colleagues and the broader community. The social cost of problem gambling was estimated at between $4.7 billion and $8.4 billion per annum by the last substantive national impact study (not including costs to the health system and welfare system that supports problem gamblers) (Productivity Commission, 2010: p. 6.36).

Gambling in Australia is controversial. More recently, concerns have been raised that wagering is becoming too closely linked to sporting activities that have traditionally been associated with family values rather than gambling. A public attitudes survey commissioned by the combined regulator overseeing telecommunications, broadcasting, radio communications and the internet, the Australian Communications and Media Authority (ACMA) [an Australian government statutory authority], found that about two-thirds (66 per cent) of Australians found promotion of betting odds during live sport broadcasts unacceptable and around six in ten (62 per cent) found advertising for betting agencies during live broadcasts unacceptable (ACMA, 2013: p. 6). The argument about normalisation refers to fears that sports betting advertising and gambling industry sponsorship erodes protection of children from gambling participation and that a culture of gambling may result in premature gambling participation and preventable harm.

Australian national reviews of television sports gambling advertising

The recent sports betting policy development process illustrates a familiar theme, of gambling industry opportunism exploiting gaps in regulation. While wagering is regulated by State/Territory laws, changes to State/Territory government betting advertising rules were triggered by the landmark 2008 High Court challenge by British company Betfair.[3] The state of Western Australia refused Betfair's application for a license to operate internet wagering, which Betfair appealed to the Australian High Court. The High Court case overturned State restrictions on betting advertisements by interstate bookmakers and the judgment invalidated specific State-based restrictions on betting exchanges, resulting in removal of restrictions on advertising by wagering providers not licensed in that jurisdiction (Loeliger, 2013; Phillips, 2013). While States assessed their legal position, withdrawal of state betting advertising restrictions left a vacuum that was filled with what many referred to as intense and repetitive or 'saturation level' sports betting advertising and the intensified involvement of corporate bookmakers[4] during Spring Racing Carnival and other major sporting events such as the Australian Football League (AFL) grand final and the Australian Tennis Open; which previously had no betting advertising. According to the Victorian Responsible Gambling Foundation (2014), there was almost five minutes of sports betting advertising per football match (Victorian Responsible Gambling Foundation, 2013: n.p.). Gambling advertising on sports betting increased 300 per cent between 2010 and 2012, and in 2012 there were 20,000 sports advertisements on free-to-air TV (Victorian Responsible Gambling Foundation, 2013a).

The potential impact of sport on advertised product market growth is significant, but at the expense of exposing under-age audiences to betting advertising during sports event broadcasts. The saturation of gambling advertising means that children come to associate gambling as an integral part of the sport (Grills, 2012); which underpins accusations that deregulation of betting advertising normalises gambling. Free TV Australia (2009: p. 30) data indicates the huge reach and potential influence of advertising during sports events, which are consistently among the top ratings programmes.[5] For example, Australian Football League premiership reached 90.4 per cent of metropolitan and 82 per cent of regional Australians, and National Rugby League premiership reached 72.8 per cent of metropolitan and 79.5 per cent of regional Australian audiences. The land-based gambling industry has also consolidated sites of gambling to include electronic gambling machines, wagering alongside TAB and now more recently, sports betting, with live sports match telecasts in alcohol-licensed venues that attract key market segments such as young men.

The Productivity Commission Report into Gambling (2010: p. 52) highlighted concerns about the exposure of children to gambling advertising and recommended a review of the 2010 Television Code of Practice exemptions relating to promotion of lotteries, Lotto, Keno and sports betting during children's viewing periods. The New South Wales Shadow Minister for Hospitality and Tourism, Racing and Major Events listed what he termed 'abuses to the principle of responsible gambling', including 'saturation' media advertising, ground signage, sports and racing commentator advertorial content (bookmakers combining sports commentary with betting odds promotions), incentives and enticements for new gamblers, credit card gambling by telephone or the internet (Productivity Commission 2010, K3 citing sub. DR379: p. 2).

Public controversy surrounding sports betting advertising triggered a series of national reviews of gambling and sports gambling-related issues and speculation on how best to regulate the industry. The Department of Broadband, Communications and the Digital Economy (DBCDE) (2012) undertook a national inquiry into the prevalence of interactive and online gambling in Australia and the adequacy of the Interactive Gambling Act 2001 and released its final report in 2012. This included: calling on the regulator, the Australian Communications and Media Authority (ACMA), to administer penalties for prohibited online activities; to minimise the risks from children's access to online betting sites; to examine legalisation of online 'in-play' betting but prohibition of 'micro betting' in sport; and development of a national harm minimisation and consumer protection framework for all forms of permissible online gambling. This would bind all providers and include harm minimisation measures such as 'pre-commitment, credit restrictions, warning messages and links to gambling helpline services' (Loeliger, 2013: n.p.). Although not specifically implicating sports advertising codes, the relevance to prevention of corruption in sport was clear in the Australian Crime Commission's (ACC) (2013) report into links between performance-enhancing drug use, organised crime and possible betting corruption in sport in Australia.

The Australian Parliamentary Joint Select Committee on Gambling Reform (PJSCGR) undertook national reviews with public submissions and published successive reports concerning online gambling and broadcasting regulation (PJSCGR, 2011; 2013). They observed that 'live odds has been seen as particularly problematic and intrusive' (PJSCGR, 2013: p. 19) (referring to changing of betting odds during game play) and were critical of the role of advertising in promoting gambling among children and vulnerable people, including problem gamblers. The Committee recommended a national regulatory framework and review of the exceptions for gambling advertising during sports broadcasts and 'a total ban of the promotion of live odds both at venues and during the broadcast of a sporting event' (PJSCOGR, 2011: p. xx). Their second report proposed a ban on gambling advertising during times when children are likely to be watching, including sports broadcasts (PJSCOGR, 2011: p. 37). They recommended further investigation and research on the long-term effects of normalisation of gambling advertising on children and called for a review of industry self-regulation: 'if industry does not make appropriate changes regarding the promotion of gambling products in an environment which includes children' (PJSCOGR, 2011: p. ix).

Research conducted for the regulator, ACMA, in 2013 ahead of bans on live odds promotion (changing betting odds during game play) during sports broadcasts, consistently found 60-plus per cent of Australians regard both presentation of betting odds and advertising by betting agencies during sports broadcasts as unacceptable, 78–85 per cent were supportive of restrictions on such practices, including Australians who bet on sports, with around 60 per cent supporting 24-hour bans (ACMA, 2013: pp.3–4).

In response, restrictions on advertising gambling services during live sports broadcasts were registered in amendments to the Commercial Television Code of Practice 2010 and the Subscription Narrowcast Television Code of Practice 2013 in July 2013 by the ACMA.

The detail of the amended codes reveals the piecemeal outcomes, which:

- prohibit the promotion of betting odds from the start until the end of play (there are limited exemptions including for the broadcast of multi-day sports and overseas live sport);
- prohibit commentators from promoting betting odds during play, and for 30 minutes before and 30 minutes after the game;
- restrict generic gambling advertisements to before and after play, scheduled breaks in play and when play is suspended;
- require gambling representatives to be clearly identified at all times;
- prohibit gambling advertising that involves a gambling representative at or around, or appearing to be at or around, the ground at any time;
- prohibit gambling representatives appearing as part, or a guest, of the commentary team at any time. (ACMA, 2013b)

Advertisements for gambling are permitted at all these times except during play (Free TV, 2010, amended July 2013, p. 42). Different rules apply to 'long form' (live sporting events, such as tennis and golf (Free TV 2010, amended July 2013, p. 42).

Reactions to the proposed code amendments was mixed. ACMA considered it had worked with industry and consulted the community.

Under guidance from COAG (Council of Australian Governments), 'industry would be provided with the opportunity to address the issue through amendments to their existing industry codes' (ACMA, 2013b, n.p.). ACMA had adopted a process of working with 'broadcasting industry bodies to develop the principles that would guide these codes' (ACMA, 2013b).

> In May 2013, in response to increasing community concern, the former Prime Minister broadened the scope of the Federal Government's policy, including to cover generic gambling advertisements (in addition to promotion of odds) and restrict the appearance and participation of representatives from gambling organisations during broadcasts of live sporting events. (ACMA, 2013b)

Gambling advertising during sports broadcasting was partially addressed through the ban of live odds advertising during live sports broadcasts, regulated through industry codes of practice, but the Free TV Code is self-serving (as this peak body represents the commercial free-to-air industry), with the regulator ACMA, tied into a protocol saying the code is adequate and that enough community consultation has taken place.

Under rather limp provisions, the ACMA must register a code of practice if it is satisfied that:

- the code contains appropriate community safeguards for the matters covered by the code;
- the code is endorsed by a majority of broadcasters to which it applies;
- members of the public have had an adequate opportunity to comment on it. (ACMA, 2013b)

Clearly, having 'adequate opportunity to comment' on a specific code is not the same as proactively eliciting and responding to continuing public criticism of sports betting advertising during family viewing of sporting events or commissioning independent research on what the public wants. The compromised outcomes were widely criticised by politicians, community organisations and gambling treatment professionals.

> If any government, State or Federal, thinks a ban on live odds will solve the problem they are treating us all as mug punters. (Xenophon, 2013)

The current gambling legislation is inadequate to protect children from the risks of acculturation into gambling activities while watching sports broadcasts. (Victorian InterChurch Gambling Taskforce, 2014: 5)

Australian Psychology Society's (APS) published an opinion on the reforms:

Gambling advertising during sporting matches and related broadcasting should be seriously restricted if not banned, with restrictions similar to those for alcohol and smoking advertising to protect vulnerable groups from exposure to gambling inducements, dissociate sport from gambling, and restore the integrity of sporting codes. (Gridley, 2013: n.p.)

Subsequently, a new Commercial Television Industry Code of Practice was developed by FreeTV (with an eight-week public submission window), registered by the regulator (ACMA) on 10 November 2015 and subject to review in early 2017 (ACMA, 2015; ACMA, 2015b). The new code shifted to 'less restrictive time zones', with changes permitting PG (parental guidance) programmes all day and earlier M (mature) and MA15+ (mature audiences) time zones than previously. The code explicitly refers to shared responsibility between government, industry and viewers 'designed to assist them to better manage their own viewing' (ACMA, 2015b).

How such outcomes were achieved where many public concerns remained unaddressed can perhaps be interpreted as the outcome of a well-organised campaign by industry to influence policy outcomes. This entails a range of strategies that is clarified by the application of CPA in the next section.

The application of CPA (corporate political activity) framework to Australian sports broadcasting policy reforms 2008–2015

Public interest integrity of operations is expected of government, the regulator and industry. How this is articulated is subject to public debate and political influence. A key issue is whether corporate political activity (CPA) undermines public interest integrity of decision-makers. The CPA framework is adapted from the analysis of CPA of the tobacco industry (Savell et al., 2013).

The reforms focused on brokered compromises in the Broadcasting Act amendments (the Broadcasting Services Act 1992 is the main

92 *Linda Hancock*

legislation controlling advertising in Australia at a federal level). The compromised outcomes raise the issue of industry influence in brokering national legislation that does not address public concerns about sports gambling advertising, that fails to take proactive protection of vulnerable persons (including minors, problem gamblers, recovering problem gamblers and the mentally challenged) and that puts in place Codes of Conduct that ignore public calls for a total ban on advertising or at least stopping the current exemption for sporting events to gambling advertising prohibitions.

The analysis of political power and influence is at the crux of these questions. Building on the work of Hilmer and Hitt (1999), Savelle et al. (2014) outline six long-term strategies used by the tobacco industry to influence public policy: Information strategy, Financial incentive strategy, Constituency building strategy, Policy substitution strategy, Legal strategy, Constituency fragmentation and Destabilisation strategy. The strength of this approach is that by applying the framework, the additive and cumulative impact of such tactics can lay bare the influence of powerful corporations; analogous to the 'emperor with no clothes'. These are applied below to illustrate how CPA thinking can be applied to the analysis of the Australian example of sports gambling industry influence over Australian broadcasting policies.

Application of CPA to the Australian sports broadcasting policy reforms 2013–2015 illustrates how:

- Industry *information strategies* seek to frame (and limit) outcomes and the range of issues under consideration. For example, Sportsbet argued there is no evidence to show the relationship between gambling advertising and problem gambling (Sportsbet Pty Ltd, 2013: p. 2). Moreover, the framing of the policy outcome as a brokered compromise focused on gambling as a social problem, serves to deflect attention from broader negative integrity issues linking sports betting to corruption within sport. (Parliamentary Joint Select Committee on Gambling Reform, 2013)
- *Financial incentive strategies*, such as taxation, sponsorships and advertising revenue, pose conflict of interest issues for the government; (Garitos, 2013; ACMA and PwC, 2014; Australian Wagering Council [AWC], 2013) and for commercial television industry peak bodies such as Free TV, which develop industry Codes and run the public submission process.
- *constituency building strategies* link gambling providers to political parties via donations and do more to unite rather than fragment the gambling industry (in this case in collaboration with commercial

TV, broadcasting, advertising and marketing interests) as a powerful lobby (Australian Electoral Commission [AEC], 2014).
- Using *policy substitution strategies*, the industry extolls the virtues of consumer choice and free markets over regulation and promotes industry self-regulation over more invasive government-enforced regulations (ACMA, 2013). The industry has systematically supported publicly funded problem gambling help TV advertising, which reinforces an individual choice/blame for problem gambling, rather than a structural interests perspective which may also bear mixed messages in terms of harm prevention and normalisation of gambling (Productivity Commission, 2010). Gambling and sports betting is embedded and normalised in sports entertainment via the brokered compromise in the reform outcomes. Industry acceptance of a ban on live odds betting substituted for acceptance of other betting promotions (such as credit upon sign-up) and legitimation of generalised gambling advertising during sporting events.
- *Legal strategies* supported by well-resourced gambling industry multinational corporations are used to win national regulatory victories (such as the High Court case brought by Betfair 2008) that open up new markets to the industry, with opportunistic advertising put hastily into place following the court decision. Soft regulation via industry-constructed codes endorsed by ACMA, Broadcasting Law and COAG (The National Council of Australian Governments), have legitimated codes that are self-serving to pro-gambling advertising industry interests.
- *Constituency fragmentation and destabilisation strategy* results in complex compromises, split allegiances and conflicts of interest. The policy outcomes do not really address the public interest issues at hand and deliver compromises that support industry interests. Framing of the issue during 2013–2015 debates in terms of live odds betting, deflected debate from the broader issue of a total ban on gambling advertisements. As Australian Churches Gambling Taskforce chairman Tim Costello explained: 'People are very clear, they're saying we're sick of gambling ads being seen by our kids, not just live odds' (Aston, 2013). Meanwhile, the Government said it needs further research to act more definitively (Gillard and Conroy, 26 May 2013).

In the Australian examination of sports betting advertising during the 2013–2015 reforms, the compromise outcome was messy and difficult to regulate, with the outcome essentially in the interests of industry. Policy bans of betting odds during sports matches, but still allowing generic gambling advertising before or after a game; or during a scheduled break in play, including a quarter-time and half-time (Maiden 2013: p. 1) essentially put in place a co-regulatory arrangement where enforcement is complex and untested.[6] In light of 2014 Federal Government budget cuts of $3.3 million over four years to ACMA (Swan and Knott, 2014), there have also been doubts about the capacity of the regulator to monitor industry codes. The risk is that self-regulation by industry compromises public interest integrity outcomes.

Since these reforms, public criticism of sports advertising during broadcast sports events has continued and the need for consistency of online and broadcast content has resulted in new government regulations. Amid a backlash from the big sporting codes, on 6 May 2017, the Australian Government announced a package of reforms including restrictions on gambling advertising during live sporting events across broadcast and online platforms (but not applying to racing). Consistent with financial and substitution strategies, they 'faced a backlash from executives of some of the nation's biggest sporting codes, who argued restricting gambling advertising would slash the value of the television rights their codes attract' (Doran, 2017).

With implementation of these reforms, since the end of March 2018, gambling advertisements have been banned from all live sport broadcasts between 5:00am and 8:30pm. However, there is a controversial exception for subscription channels that are deemed to have a 'low-audience share', which can continue to market betting products during these times. The partial restriction to 8.30pm also means that sports betting advertising is allowed from that time up until 4am (McIvor, 2018), which assumes that children are not using multimedia after 8.30pm. It is only strident and persistent public complaints that have forced the hand of the regulator, but the strength of the gambling industry lobby continues to result in gaps in regulation that defeat the overall purpose of the legislation – which is to minimise harm to minors and other vulnerable persons and address the gaps initially created by the 2008 High Court judgment.

Conclusion

Sports betting continues to be a rapidly growing and developing market in Australia and in other jurisdictions such as the UK, Canada and New Zealand, with strong competition between domestic and international corporate bookmakers and betting agencies.

This chapter focuses on integrity issues in relation to sports betting, online gambling and youth, focusing on the impact of sports betting advertising on children and the complexities of regulation. Set within an international context, it first briefly explains changing technology and the heightened risks of online gambling; the vulnerability of youth to gambling-related harms and the impact of gambling advertising on youth. The examination of the reform process of broadcasting laws and industry codes on gambling advertising, relates to government response to public controversy raised by 'saturated' sports betting following the 2008 Betfair Australian High Court decision, when State governments' withdrawal of advertising regulation created a regulatory vacuum. Betfair opened up new opportunities for the gambling industry, marked by the involvement of globalised transnational corporations, adept at finding new markets and negotiating regulatory concessions, using a toolbox of well-established strategies that become evident using CPA analysis. The case prompts a number of questions of the Australian reform process. CPA analysis of the politics of government regulation of sports betting advertising is a window into understanding how the gambling industry has sought to influence government via industry strategies to broker outcomes in favour of industry interests.

The Parliament has the power, through s.128 of the Broadcasting Services Act 1992, to directly amend the existing codes of practice for broadcasting, which it has done, but in ways that did not address critics arguing against betting advertising during sporting events. As the legal company Holding Redlich observed regarding the aftermath of the decision:

> It was inevitable that this saturation marketing of gambling would result in burgeoning public concern with regard to the welfare of vulnerable groups, such as children and those with a gambling problem. Of course increased gambling in sport also leads to increased speculation around tampering and the integrity of those affected sports more generally. (Loeliger, 2013: p. 1)

Many saw the reform process post-Betfair as a lost opportunity to address the key public issues of exposure of youth to gambling advertising. Policies overlooked in the process could have drawn on public health models to include additional measures such as banning advertising by any online gaming providers; adopting measures to block or interrupt the access to illegal offshore providers (Liberal Party of Australia, 2013: p. 6); mandating player limit-setting prior to playing/betting online; and potential in-ground and sponsorship regulatory changes.

The role of government is to ensure integrity in the public interest. In ensuring the integrity of gambling operator's license to operate, governments use a range of instruments including legislation, regulation and co-regulation through industry codes of practice. On the continuum of regulatory enforcement, industry codes are noted for their potential 'light touch regulation', as the efficacy of their enforcement depends on both the content of the code and the extent to which industry compliance is regulated, monitored and enforced (Hancock, 2011; Hancock and Smith, 2017a, b). The reforms basically left the industry to self-regulate in the context of a regulator left with a complicated regulatory field and diminished resources.

As the examples above illustrate, the power of vested financial and political interests have trumped public concerns about the creeping expansion of gambling and the use of saturation-level advertising into TV sports betting during family viewing of sporting events in Australia. Public reaction to the rapid and visible increase in sports betting advertising disrupted the prevailing co-regulatory model of State/Territory governments acting through shared interests with industry (based on state revenue/industry profit), but the reform process reproduced pro-industry compromise at the national level as the outcome of a national review process. In comparison with the trade-offs brokered by these vested interests, public concerns have taken second place.

This chapter has charted some of the integrity challenges of sports betting regulation. Vulnerable groups (minors and existing and recovering problem gamblers) could be spared from exposure to gambling-related normalisation and potential risk and harm by national bans on TV sports betting or more broadly, a blanket ban on advertising across all forms of gambling and bans on indirect advertising through sponsorships. The focus on attempts in Australia to ban gambling advertising during sports television broadcasts and the resulting pro-industry compromises, show that the struggle involves powerful vested interests and high-level political alliances, and is likely to be drawn-out.

Acknowledgments

Funding for this research from Australian Research Council (ARC) Linkage Grant (LP130100046).

Notes

1 In Canada for example, they found that 'net monthly gambling expenditure is $541.09 compared to $67.09 for Non-Internet gamblers. Internationally, the figures are $195.14 and $19.26 respectively' (Wood and Williams, 2009: p. 9).
2 This is considerably higher compared to other countries such as New Zealand ($495 per capita), Canada ($393 per capita) and the United States ($325 per capita) (Delfabbro, 2010).

3 *Betfair Pty Limited v Western Australia* (2008) 234 CLR 418.
4 Major corporate bookmakers in Australia include: Sportsbet, Betchoice, Betezy, Betstar, Centrebet, Centreracing, Luxbet, Overtheodds, Sportingbet Australia and Sports Alive (Productivity Commission, 2010: p. 16.6).
5 In 2006 10 of the top 20 programmes were sport (Free TV Australia 2009: p. 26).
6 Continued use of industry codes is consistent with the decision of the Council of Australian Governments (COAG) in 2011 to allow industry the opportunity to self-regulate. Direct regulation is not consistent with COAG's stance of May 2011 to explore industry self-regulatory options (ACMA, 2013b).

References

Aston, H. (2013). 'TV can't afford gambling ad ban: Conroy', *The Sydney Morning Herald*, 25 May. Accessed 4 June 2017, www.smh.com.au/federal-politics/political-news/tv-cant-afford-gambling-ad-ban-conroy-20130527-2n7k6.html

Australian Clearinghouse for Youth Studies (ACYS) (2013). *Youth Gambling in Australia* [Online]. ACYS. Accessed 13 May 2016 at: www.acys.info/facts/gambling

Australian Communications and Media Authority (ACMA) (2013). *Betting Odds and Advertising for Betting Agencies During Sports Broadcasts: Community Research*, Australian Government – Australian Communications and Media Authority. Accessed 27 July 2017 at: www.acma.gov.au/~/media/mediacomms/Report/pdf/Community_attitudes_to_live_odds_and_sport_pdf1 pdf.pdf

Australian Communications and Media Authority (ACMA) (2013b). *Betting Sports odds and gambling codes registered*. Accessed 15 November 2016 at: www.acma.gov.au/theACMA/Newsroom/Newsroom/Media-releases/betting-odds-and-gambling-codes-registered

Australian Communications and Media Authority (ACMA) (2015). *Commercial_Television_Industry_Code_of_Practice*. Accessed 5 December 2016 at: www.acma.gov.au/~/media/Broadcasting%20Investigations/Regulation/pdf/Commercial_Television_Industry_Code_of_Practice_2015%20pdf.PDF

Australian Communications and Media Authority (ACMA) (2015b). *The ACMA Registers New Commercial Television Industry Code of Practice, 10 November*. Accessed 15 December 2017 at: www.acma.gov.au/Industry/Broadcast/Television/TV-content-regulation/the-acma-registers-new-commercial-television-industry-code-of-practice

Australian Communications and Media Authority (ACMA) and PriceWaterhouseCooper (Pwc) (2014). *The Cost of Code Interventions on Commercial Broadcasters*. Accessed 26 June 2016 at: www.acma.gov.au/theACMA/Library/researchacma/Research-reports/acma-research-and-publications-1

Australian Crime Commission (ACC) (2013). *Threats to the Integrity of Professional Sport in Australia.* Accessed 21 June 2017 at: www.crimecommission.gov.au/publications/intelligence-products/crime-profile-fact-sheets/threats-integrity-professional-sport

Australian Electoral Commission (2014). 'Home – Annual Returns. Accessed 30 June 2014 at: http://periodicdisclosures.aec.gov.au

Australian Liberal Party (2013). *Helping Problem Gamblers.* Accessed 20 June 2014 at: www.liberal.org.au/helping-problem-gamblers

Australian Wagering Council (AWC) (2013). *Submission to the Independent Gambling Authority (IGA) regarding the proposed Advertising Code Of Practice (Live Odds) Variation Notice 2013 (Draft Live Odds Notice).* Accessed 25 June 2014 at: http://australianwageringcouncil.com/assets/AWC_Final_Submission_SA_IGA_130625.pdf

Betfair (2008). *Betfair Pty Limited v Western Australia* (2008) 234 CLR 418

Bolton Council (2012). *Bolton Council Statement of Principles.* Accessed 23 June 2014 at: www.google.co.uk/url?sa=t&rct=j&q=&esrc=s&source=web&cd=1&ved=0CCEQFjAA&url=http%3A%2F%2Fwww.bolton.gov.uk%2Fsites%2FDocumentCentre%2FDocuments%2FGambling%2520Act%2520Statement%2520of%2520Princplies%25202013-2016.doc&ei=9WZLVKajNMOR7AaV6oHgCg&usg=AFQjCNHPdJfS00cJbbBOsegZ74w0lAlXQg&bvm=bv.77880786,d.ZWU

Chapman, J. (2015). TV betting adverts viewed by children split the Coalition: Row over whether to lift restrictions on commercials. *The Daily Mail.* Accessed 5 June 2015, at: www.dailymail.co.uk/news/article-2919133/TV-betting-adverts-viewed-children-split-Coalition-Row-lift-restrictions-commercials.htm

Delfabbro, P. H. (2010). Exploring the myths around gambling. Paper presented at *Gambling Awareness Week*, Melbourne Town Hall, Melbourne.

Delfabbro, P., Lambos, C., King, D. and Puglies, S. (2009). 'Knowledge and beliefs about gambling in Australian secondary school students and their implications for education strategies'. *Journal of Gambling Studies*, 4, pp. 523–529.

Department of Broadband Communications and the Digital Economy (DBCDE) (2012). *Review of the Interactive Gambling Act 2001 Final Report.* Accessed 20 June 2014 at: www.communications.gov.au/__data/assets/pdf_file/0007/162277/Final_Report_-_Review_of_the_Interactive_Gambling_Act_2001.pdf

Deverensky, J., Sklar, J., Gupta, R. and Messerlian, C. (2010). An empirical study examining the impact of gambling advertising on adolescent gambling attitudes and behaviours. *International J Mental Health Addiction*, 8, pp. 21–34.

Doran, M. (2017). Gambling advertising to be banned during live sporting events, *ABC News*, 6 May. Accessed 11 April 2018 at: www.abc.net.au/news/2017-05-06/gambling-ads-during-live-sporting-events-to-be-banned/8502524

European Commission (2014). Online gambling: Commission recommends principles to ensure effective protection of consumers. Accessed at: http://europa.eu/rapid/press-release_IP-14-828_en.htm

European Parliament (2009). *European Parliament Resolution of 10 March 2009 on the Integrity of Online Gambling* (2008/2215(INI)), para I. Accessed 2 June 2014 at: www.europarl.europa.eu/sides/getDoc.do?type=TA&language=EN&reference=P6-TA-2009-97

European Parliament (2013). Texts adopted: Online Gambling in the online market. 14 July. Accessed 3 June 2017 at: www.europarl.europa.eu/sides/getDoc.do?pubRef=-//EP//TEXT+TA+P7-TA-2013-0348+0+DOC+XML+V0//en

European Parliament (2018). (updated) 2012/2322(INI) – 23/10/2012 Non-legislative basic document. Accessed at: www.europarl.europa.eu/oeil/popups/summary.do?id=1238045&t=e&l=en

Free TV Australia (2009). *Submission to the Department of Broadband, Communications and the Digital Economy, Sport on Television: A review of the anti-siphoning scheme in the contemporary digital environment*, Free TV Australia. Accessed 15 December 2013 at: www.freetv.com.au/media/Submissions/2009-0014_SUB_Antisiphoning_Sport_on_TV_review_Free_TV_Australia_161009.pdf

Fried, B. G., Teichman, M. and Raha, G. (2010). 'Adolescent gambling: Temperament, sense of coherence and exposure to advertising'. *Addiction Research and Theory*, 18, pp. 586–598.

Gainsbury, S., Hing, N., Blaszczynski, A. and Wood, R. (2011). *An investigation of Internet gambling in Australia*. Lismore, NSW, Australia: Southern Cross University, Centre for Gambling Education & Research.

Garlitos, K. (2013). *Gambling TV ad ban will cost networks loads of money*, Calvinayre. Accessed 14 June 2014 at: http://calvinayre.com/2013/05/28/business/gambling-tv-ad-ban-will-cost-networks-loads-of-money/

Gillard, J. and Conroy, S. (2013). 'Betting Odds Advertising Banned during the Broadcast of Live Sports Matches', *Joint Media Release*, 26 May 2013, Government of Australia.

Gridley, H. (2013). The increasing harm from advertising and promotion of gambling in sport. *InPsych*, June APS accessed 15 June 2017 at: www.psychology.org.au/publications/inpsych/2013/june/gambling/

Griffiths, M. D. (2003). Does Gambling Advertising Contribute to Problem Gambling? Paper presented to the *World Lottery Association Conference*, London, England, September.

Griffiths, M. (2007). Does gambling advertising contribute to problem gambling? *International Journal of Mental Health and Addiction*, 3(2), 15–25.

Grills, N. (2012). New Challenges in Public Health Practice: The Ethics of Industry Alliance with Health Promoting Charities. *Public Health – Methodology, Environmental and Systems Issues*. doi:10.5772/36204

Hancock, L. (2011). *Regulatory Failure: The Case of Crown Casino*, Melbourne: Australian Scholarly Publishing.

Hancock, L. and Smith, G. (2017a). Replacing the Reno Model with a Robust Public Health Approach to Responsible Gambling: Hancock and Smith's Response to Commentaries on Our Original Reno Model Critique. *International Journal of Mental Health and Addiction*, *15*(3) 1209–1220.

Hancock, L. and Smith, G. (2017b). Critiquing the Reno Model I-IV international influence on regulators and governments (2004–2015) – the distorted reality of Responsible gambling. *International Journal of Mental Health and Addiction*, *15*(3).

Hillman, A. and Hitt, M. (1999). Corporate political Strategy formulation: A model of approach, participation and strategy decisions. *The Academy of Management Review*, *24*(4), 825–842.

Hinn, N., Sprotson, K., Brading, R. and Brook, K. (2014). *Review and Analysis of Sports and Race Betting Inducements*. Melbourne, Australia: Victorian Responsible Gambling Foundation.

Loeliger, J. (2013). Advertising and promotion of gambling in sport', *Holding Redlich Update*, 3 July. Accessed 30 June 2016 at: www.holdingredlich.com/assets/docs/Advertising%20final%203%20July.pdf

Maiden, S. (2013). 'Julia Gillard to ban Tom Waterhouse and other bookies from broadcasts'. *The Daily Telegraph*, 26 May. Accessed 30 May 2016 at: www.dailytelegraph.com.au/news/nsw/julia-gillard-to-ban-tom-waterhouse-and-other-bookies-from-broadcasts/story-fni0cx12-1226650572977

McGaurr, L. (2013). *Youth Gambling in Australia*, Australian Clearing House for Youth Studies. Accessed 30 May 2016 at: www.acys.info/facts/gambling/FTF_Gambling_briefing.pdf

McIvor, D. (2018). NBA play-offs coverage reveals gap in gambling ad restrictions targeting kids, *ABC News*. Accessed at: www.abc.net.au/news/2018-05-08/nba-play-offs-coverage-reveals-sports-betting-ad-loophole/9736060

McMullan, J. L., Miller, D. E. and Perrier, D. C. (2012). I've seen them so much they are just there: Exploring young people's perceptions of gambling in advertising'. *International Journal of Mental Health and Addiction*, *10*(6), pp. 829–848.

Messerlian, C., Derevensky, J. and Gupta, R. (2005). Youth gambling problems: A public health perspective. *Health Promotion International*, *20*(1): 69–79.

Monaghan, S. (2008). An appraisal of the impact of the depiction of gambling in society on youth. *International Journal of Mental Health & Addiction*, 6, 537–550.

Monaghan, S., Derevensky, J. and Sklar, A. (2008). Impact of gambling advertisements and marketing on children and adolescents: Policy recommendations to minimize harm. *Journal of Gambling Issues*, 22, pp. 252–274.

Ontario Problem Gambling Research Centre (2013). Facts about sports betting in Ontario. Accessed 24 May 2015 at: www.problemgambling.ca/EN/Documents/FA_SportsBetting2013.pdf

Parliamentary Joint Select Committee on Gambling Reform (PJSCOGR) (2011). *Parliamentary Joint Select Committee on Gambling Reform Second* report *Interactive and online gambling and gambling advertising.* [Online] Accessed 13 January 2014 at: www.aph.gov.au/~/media/wopapub/senate/committee/gamblingreform_ctte/completed_inquires/2010-13/interactive_online_gambling_advertising/report/report.ashx

Parliamentary Joint Select Committee on Gambling Reform (PJSCOGR) (2013). The advertising and promotion of gambling services in sport. Accessed 30 August 2015 at: www.aph.gov.au/~/media/wopapub/senate/committee/gamblingreform_ctte/completed_inquires/2010-13/gambling_sport/report/report.ash

Parliament of Australia (2013b). Submissions received by the Committee. Accessed 15 July 2014 at: www.aph.gov.au/Parliamentary_Business/Committees/Joint/Former_Committees/gamblingreform/completedinquires/2010-13/gamblingsport/submissions

Phillips, T. (2013). *Gambling and Young People: Impacts, Challenges and Responses*, The Victorian Responsible Gambling Foundation. Accessed 30 June 2014 at: http://kidbet.com.au/download/Gambling%20and%20young%20people.PDF

Productivity Commission (2010). *Inquiry Report: Gambling.* Melbourne: Productivity Commission.

Queensland Government Statistician's Office, Queensland Treasury (2017). *Australian Gambling Statistics*, 33rd edition. Accessed at: www.qgso.qld.gov.au/products/reports/aus-gambling-stats/aus-gambling-stats-33rd-edn-summary-tables.pdf

Responsible Gambling Advocacy Centre (RGAC) (2011). *Discussion Paper – Online Gambling: The State of Play. Accessed May 14 2014 at:* www.responsiblegambling.vic.gov.au/__data/assets/pdf_file/0016/8053/RGAC-Discussion-Paper-Online-Gambling-State-of-Play.pdf

Savell, E., Gilmore, A. B. & Fooks, G. (2014). How does the tobacco industry attempt to influence marketing regulations? A systematic review. *PLoS ONE.* 2014; 9(2):e87389.

Seccombe, M. (2014). Betting against political resolve on gambling, *The Saturday Paper.* Accessed 28 September at: www.thesaturdaypaper.com.au/news/politics/2014/09/27/betting-against-political-resolve-gambling/14117400001041#.VE4TnUuQw0w

Sportsbet Pty Ltd (2013). *Submission of Sportsbet Pty Ltd to Parliamentary Joint Select Committee on Gambling Reform Inquiry into the advertising and promotion of gambling services in sport.* [Online] Accessed 15 July 2014 at: www.aph.gov.au/Parliamentary_Business/Committees/Joint/Former_Committees/gamblingreform/completedinquires/2010-13/gamblingsport/submissions

Swan, J. & Knott, M. (2014). *Federal budget 2014*, 13 May. Accessed 30 May 2016, from *The Sydney Morning Herald* at: www.smh.com.au/national/federal-budget-2014-abc-sbs-cut-by-435-million-20140513-3882s.html

The Social Research Centre (2013). *Gambling Prevalence in South Australia.* Adelaide: Office for Problem Gambling.

Thomas, S., Pitt, H., Bestman, A., Randle, M., Daube, M. & Pettigrew, S. (2016). *Child and Parent Recall of Gambling Sponsorship in Australian Sport*. Melbourne: Victorian Responsible Gambling Foundation.

Thomas, S. (2013). Gambling and young people: impacts, challenges and responses. *Victorian Responsible Gambling Foundation*, 1(1).

Victorian InterChurch Gambling Taskforce (2014). Jackpot for the Pokies industry. Accessed 6 July 2014 at: http://churchgamblingtaskforce.wordpress.com/

Victorian Responsible Gambling Foundation (2013a). Media Release. Gambling's Not a Game, 9 October 2014. Accessed 29 April 2014 at: www.responsiblegambling.vic.gov.au/newsroom/media-releases/2013/gamblings-not-a-game-highlights-gambling-risks-to-kids

Victorian Responsible Gambling Foundation (2013b). *Responsible Gambling Awareness Week: The Changing Gambling Environment*. Accessed 29 April 2014 at: www.rgaw.com.au/changing-gambling-environment

Wood, R. T. and Williams, R. J. (2009). *Internet Gambling: Prevalence, Patterns, Problems, and Policy Options*. Final Report prepared for the Ontario Problem Gambling Research Centre, Guelph, Ontario, Canada. 5 January 2009.

Xenophon (2013). 'Live Odds', *Nick Xenophon Blog*. Accessed 15 July 2014 at: www.nickxenophon.com.au/nicks-blog/live-odds/

Index

Note: page numbers in *italic* type refer to Figures; those in **bold** type refer to Tables.

ACC (Australian Crime Commission) 88
ACMA (Australian Communications and Media Authority) 86, 88, 89–90, 91, 93, 94
addiction *see* problem gambling
advertising *see* Australia, sports betting advertising
Advertising and Promotion of Gambling Services in Sport (Parliament of Australia) 79
AFL (Australian Football League) 87
age limits in gambling 82
Alberta, Canada, gambling regulation 11, **15**, 16
Alcohol and Gaming Commission, Nova Scotia, Canada 11
Alcohol and Gaming Commission, Ontario, Canada 12
American Municipal Association 68–69
Anti-Corruption Summit, London 2016 76–77
APS (Australian Psychology Society) 91
Asia, gambling industry 73–74
Atlantic Lottery Corporation, Canada 9, 10, 11
ATP (Association of Tennis Professionals) 46
Australia: internet gambling 84, 85
Australia, sports betting advertising in 3–4, 79–80, 82, 84, 94–96; age limits in gambling 82; CPA (corporate political activity) analysis of policy reforms 2008–2015 80–81, 91–94, 95; national reviews of television advertising 86–91; regulatory context 85–86
Australian Churches Gambling Taskforce 93
Australian Open (tennis) 47, 87
Austria, gambling regulation 31

Baseball World Series, 1919 70
BCLC (British Columbia Lottery Corporation) 11–12
Belgium: gambling regulation 31; Ladbrokes in 34–35, 36; lottery 2
Betfair 46; Australian High Court case 87, 93, 95
Betfred.com 48
Bill C-190, Canada 21–22, 24
'black market' operators 29; *see also* illegal gambling
British Columbia, Canada, gambling regulation 11–12, **15**
Broadcasting Services Act 1992, Australia 91–92, 93, 95
Burnett, Jamie 55

Calgary Winter Olympic Games, 1988 6
Cameron, David 76

Index

Canada: age limits in gambling 82; gambling advertising 83; internet gambling 80–81
Canada, sports betting regulation in 2; and Canadian federalism 6–7; coherence of regulations 16–20, *18*, *19*, *20*, *21*, *22*, **23**; development of 5–6; future developments 20–22, 24; regulatory framework 7–12, **13–15**, 16, *16*
Carpenter, K. 51
casino games, illegal 28, 29
certification systems 36–37, 38
Challenger Tour 53, 54
Chambers, S. 53
Chappelet, J-L. 43
Charitable (Ch) model of regulation 2, 9, 10, 12, **13–15**, 16, *16*
children *see* minors, protection of
China, gambling industry 67
Chrétien, Jean 7
COAG (Council of Australian Governments) 90, 93
Comartin, Joe 21–22, 24
Commercial Television Code of Practice 2010, Australia 89
Commercial Television Industry Code of Practice, Australia 91
constituency building strategies (CPA analysis) 92–93
constituency fragmentation and destabilisation strategies (CPA analysis) 93
Constitutional Act 1867, Canada 7
corporate social responsibility/ performance 33; *see also* social responsibility of sports betting operators
Costello, Frank 69–70
Costello, Tim 93
Council of Europe 43, 56
'courtsiding' 47
CPA (corporate political activity) analysis of Australian sports betting advertising policy reforms 2008–2015 80–81, 91–94, 95
Criminal Code, Canada 5, 6, 7–9; Bill C-190 21–22, 24
criminal organisations *see* organised crime
cycling, and Germany 57–58

Davydenko, Nikolay 45
DBCDE (Department of Broadband, Communications and the Digital Economy), Australia 88
Department of Justice and Public Safety, Prince Edward Island, Canada 11, 18
Department of Public Safety, Newfoundland and Labrador, Canada 11, 18
drug monies 66; *see also* money laundering
Dwyer, William 'Big' 70

economic benefits of gambling 28, 29–30
episodic games 52–53
EU: Expert Group on Good Governance in Sport 58; gambling market value 28
Europe, sports betting market 44–45
European Commission 56
European Lotteries (EL) Responsible Gaming Standard 36
European Parliament, Integrity of Online Gambling resolution 81–82

FATF (Financial Action Task Force) 3, 65, 72–74
Federal Wire Act of 1961, US 71
federalism, in Canada 2, 6–7
Federer, Roger 44
Feutsel, E. 51
FIFA: and gambling corruption 44; World Cup 42
financial dimension of performance measurement 27, 32
financial flows, illicit 66; *see also* money laundering
financial incentive strategies (CPA analysis) 92
football: gambling corruption 28, 44; Italy 57; money-laundering 3, 65, 72–74
Football Association 54–55
Free TV Australia 87, 91
Free TV Code, Australia 90

Gambling Act 2005 (UK) 30, 82
gambling addiction *see* problem gambling

Gambling Commission (UK) 51, 75, 81–82
Gaming and Liquor Act, Alberta, Canada 11
Gaming and Liquor Commission, Alberta, Canada 11
Gaming Control Branch, Department of Public Safety, New Brunswick, Canada 11
Gaming Policy and Enforcement Branch, Ministry of Finance, British Columbia, Canada 11
gender, and prize money 58
Germany: cycling 57–58; sports betting market 44
'Good Governance and Ethics in Sport' (Council of Europe Parliamentary Assembly) 43
government funding of major sports events 42
Government Ownership and Control model of regulation 2, 9, 10, 12, **13–15**, *16*
'grey market' operators 29; *see also* illegal gambling
Gunn, B. 45

Harris, N. 50–51
Holding Redlich 95
Hoover, J. Edgar 70
Hruby, P. 57

ICSS (International Centre for Sport Security) 50
illegal gambling 28–29, 36; Canada 19–20
information strategies (CPA analysis) 92
inside information, and match-fixing 54–55
Interactive Gambling Act 2001, Australia 85, 88
International Boxing Council 70
International Cricket Council Anti-Corruption and Security Unit 46
International Sport Integrity Partnership 76
internet gambling 19–20, 65, 79; Australia 84, 85; Canada 80–81; and money laundering 28, 73;

Index 105

payout rates 66–67; profile of gamblers 80; technology and risks 80–82
Interpol 68, 73
Interprovincial Lottery Corporation 9
IOC (International Olympic Committee) 42
Italy, and football 57

Joint-Venture (JV) model of regulation 2, 9–10, 12, **13–15**, 16, *16*

Kefauver Committee 3, 65, 68–72
Kennedy Administration, US 70–71
Koellerer, Daniel 47
Krotiouk, Sergeo 47
Kumantsov, Andrey 47

Ladbrokes in Belgium 34–35, 36
Lamri, Morgan 47
Lee, Stephen 49, 52
legal dimension of performance measurement 27, 32
legal strategies (CPA analysis) 93
Liquor, Racing and Gambling Commission (Régie des alcools, des courses et des jeux), Québec, Canada 10
Liquor and Gaming Authority, Manitoba, Canada 11
Liquor and Gaming Authority, Saskatchewan, Canada 11
Liquor and Lotteries Corporation, Manitoba, Canada 11
live odds gambling 89
London Olympic Games, 2012 42
Loto-Québec 10, 11–12
lotteries: Canada 8–9, 10–12; certification systems 36–37, 38; illegal 28, 29
Lotteries and Gaming Corporations, New Brunswick, Canada 11
Lotteries Commissions, Prince Edward Island, Canada 11, 18
Lotto Canada 5

Macau, China: age limits in gambling 82; gambling industry 67
Maennig, W. 44
Mafia groups, US 65, 69–70

major events, economic value of 42
Manitoba, Canada, gambling regulation 11, **15**
match-fixing 2–3, 43–44; emergent patterns in 50–55, **52**; episodic games and online betting 52–53; future action against 55–59; inside information 54–55; and money laundering 3, 64–77; recommendations 75–77; reporting and prosecution 51–52; and snooker 48–50, **49**, 51–52, 53, 54, 55, 56, 57; and tennis 44–48, **45**, 50–51, 51–52, 53–54, 55, 56, 57; vulnerable players and officials 53–54
media, role in exposing match-fixing 51
minors, protection of 29; risks from online gambling 80–82; sports betting advertising, Australia 79, 86–96; vulnerability to gambling advertising and harms 82–84
money laundering 28, 50; definition 66; and match-fixing 3, 64–77; recommendations 75–77
Montreal Summer Olympic Games, 1976 5, 6
multidimensional performance measurement of sports betting operators 27–28, 31–39
Murray, Andy 52

Nadal, Rafael 44
National Hockey League 70
National Rugby League, Australia 87
NBC Universal 42
New Brunswick, Canada, gambling regulation 9, 11, **14**
Newfoundland and Labrador, Canada, gambling regulation 9, 11, **13**, 18
Norsk Tipping 31, 35–36, 38
Norway: gambling regulation 31; lottery 2
Nova Scotia, Canada, gambling regulation 9, 10–11, **13**

officials, vulnerability and match-fixing 54
Olympic Games 42; Calgary Winter Olympic Games, 1988 6; London Olympic Games, 2012 42; Montreal Olympic Games, 1976 5, 6
online gambling *see* internet gambling
Ontario, Canada, gambling regulation 12, **14**, 16, 18
Ontario Lottery and Gaming Commission, Ontario (OLG), Canada 12
Ontario Lottery and Gaming Corporation, Ontario (OLG), Canada 18
operational dimension of performance measurement 27, 32
organised crime 2–3, 28, 36, 50, 64; Kefauver Committee 3, 65, 68–72; *see also* match-fixing; money laundering
Organized Crime Control Act of 1970, US 71

payout rates 66–67
PJSCGR (Australian Parliamentary Joint Select Committee on Gambling Reform) 88–89
players and officials, vulnerability and match-fixing 53–54
policy substitution strategies (CPA analysis) 93
Prince Edward Island, Canada, gambling regulation 9, 11, **13**, 18
private sector sport-betting providers 2
prize money: and gender 58; snooker 48; tennis 53–54
problem gambling 29, 82; Australia case study 3–4, 86
Productivity Commission, Australia 82, 85, 87–88
provincial governments, Canada *see* Canada, sports betting regulation
public institution sport-betting providers 2
public values dimension of performance measurement 33

Québec, Canada 7; gambling regulation 6, 10, **14**, 16

Rebeggiani, F. 57
Rebeggiani, L. 57
Rees, J. 45, 46, 47
regulation of gambling 1–2; rationale for 28–31; regulatory scope 30; regulatory stringency 30–31; *see also* Australia, sports betting advertising; Canada, sports betting regulation
Remote Gambling Association 75
responsible gambling 27, 32, 33–38; certification systems 36–37, 38
RICO (Racketeer Influenced and Corrupt Organizations) Act of 1970, US 71
Rodenburg, R. 51
Rothenberg, B. 54, 55, 58
Rothstein, Arnold 70

Saskatchewan, Canada, gambling regulation 11, **15**, 16
Saskatchewan Indian Gaming Authority 11
Saskatchewan Lotteries 11
Savelle, E. 92
security issues in gambling 28
Service Newfoundland 18
snooker, match-fixing in 2–3, 48–50, **49**, 51–52, 53, 54, 55, 56, 57
social dimension of performance measurement *see* social responsibility of sports betting operators
social responsibility of sports betting operators 27, 32, 33–38
Social Union Framework Agreement, 1999 (Canada) 7
SportAccord 66–67
sports betting advertising, Australia *see* Australia, sports betting advertising
sports betting operators: multidimensional performance measurement 27–28, 31–39; social responsibility 27, 32, 33–38
sports officials, vulnerability and match-fixing 54
spot fixing 52–53
stakeholder dimension of performance measurement 32

Subscription Narrowcast Television Code of Practice 2013, Australia 89
Sutton, John 55
Switzerland, illegal gambling 28–29

Television Code of Practice 2010, Australia 87–88
tennis, match-fixing in 2–3, 44–48, **45**, 50–51, 51–52, 53–54, 55, 56, 57
Tennis Anti-Corruption Programme 46
Theodoraki, E. 43
Thomas, S. 83
TIU (Tennis Integrity Unit) 46–47, 48, 50, 51, 58–59
tobacco industry 92
Tour de France 58

UK: age limits in gambling 82; gambling regulation 30; sports betting advertising 83–84
Uniform Tennis Anti-Corruption Program 46–47
United Nations Convention against Transnational Organized Crime 75
United Nations Conventions against Corruption 75
United Nations Office on Drugs and Crime (UNODC) 66
University of Sydney Gambling Clinic 84
US: age limits in gambling 82; Congressional Executive Commission on China 67; Senate Special Committee to Investigate Organised Crime (*see* Kefauver Committee)

Van Rompuy, B. 57
Vassallo Arguello, Martin 45
Victorian InterChurch Gambling Taskforce 91
Victorian Responsible Gambling Foundation 83, 87

WADA (World Anti-Doping Agency) 59, 73
Western Canada Lottery Corporation 10, 11

Willerton, Nigel 47
Williams, R. J. 80
Wimbledon 44, 48; prize money 53
WLA (World Lottery Association) Responsible Gaming Framework 36, 37, 38
women, and prize money 58
Wood, R. T. 80
World Championship (snooker) 48

World's Fair, 1967 6
WPBSA (World Professional Billiards and Snooker Association) 48, 49, 50

Xenophon 90

young people *see* minors, protection of